Trauma-Sensitive
School Leadership

Trauma-Sensitive School Leadership

Building a Learning Environment to Support Healing and Success

Bill Ziegler • Dave Ramage
Andrea Parson • Justin Foster

Arlington, Virginia USA

2800 Shirlington Road, Suite 1001 • Arlington, VA 22206 USA
Phone: 800-933-2723 or 703-578-9600 • Fax: 703-575-5400
Website: www.ascd.org • Email: member@ascd.org
Author guidelines: www.ascd.org/write

Penny Reinart, *Chief Impact Officer;* Genny Ostertag, *Managing Director, Book Acquisitions & Editing;* Allison Scott, *Senior Acquisitions Editor;* Julie Houtz, *Director, Book Editing;* Katie Martin, *Editor;* Thomas Lytle, *Creative Director;* Donald Ely, *Art Director;* Georgia Park, *Senior Graphic Designer;* Cynthia Stock, *Typesetter;* Kelly Marshall, *Production Manager;* Shajuan Martin, *E-Publishing Specialist*

All web links in this book are correct as of the publication date below but may have become inactive or otherwise modified since that time. If you notice a deactivated or changed link, please email books@ascd.org with the words "Link Update" in the subject line. In your message, please specify the web link, the book title, and the page number on which the link appears.

PAPERBACK ISBN: 978-1-4166-3100-2   ASCD product #122013   n8/22
PDF EBOOK ISBN: 978-1-4166-3101-9; see Books in Print for other formats.
Quantity discounts are available: email programteam@ascd.org or call 800-933-2723, ext. 5773, or 703-575-5773. For desk copies, go to www.ascd.org/deskcopy.

Library of Congress Cataloging-in-Publication Data

Names: Ziegler, Bill, author. | Ramage, Dave, author. | Parson, Andrea, author. | Foster, Justin, author.
Title: Trauma-sensitive school leadership : building a learning environment to support healing and success / Bill Ziegler, Dave Ramage, Andrea Parson, Justin Foster.
Description: Arlington, VA : ASCD, [2022] | Includes bibliographical references and index.
Identifiers: LCCN 2022011014 (print) | LCCN 2022011015 (ebook) | ISBN 9781416631002 (paperback) | ISBN 9781416631019 (pdf)
Subjects: LCSH: Educational leadership. | School management and organization. | School environment. | School psychology. | Psychic trauma in children.
Classification: LCC LB2806 .Z494 2022 (print) | LCC LB2806 (ebook) | DDC 371.2/011—dc23/eng/20220506
LC record available at https://lccn.loc.gov/2022011014
LC ebook record available at https://lccn.loc.gov/2022011015

31 30 29 28 27 26 25 24 23 22   1 2 3 4 5 6 7 8 9 10 11 12

Trauma-Sensitive School Leadership

Introduction

We wrote this book to help school leaders create a more supportive learning environment for students living with trauma. In the chapters that follow, we highlight the principles for trauma-sensitive leadership—principles that will help you see students for who they are (rather than who you'd like them to be), reduce bias and barriers to learning in all of your school's classrooms, and build a team of dedicated educators working together to enhance student learning and well-being.

And we'll tell you right up front what the foundation for this work is: *relationships*—your relationships with students and your staff, and your teachers' relationships with the students in their classrooms.

Effective learning happens best with a social experience (Brown et al., 2014; Jensen, 2009; Lave & Wenger, 1991; Seeley-Brown & Duguid, 2002). You've probably heard the adage "no one cares how much you know until they know how much you care" used to explain why it's so essential for teachers to communicate their investment in their students' well-being. But this is equally true for any school leader who hopes to enlist the dedicated cooperation of adults learning in a community of practice.

In *Trauma-Sensitive School Leadership*, we—Bill, Dave, Andrea, and Justin—share experience-based insights drawn from our own lives as school leaders and school counselors. We don't pretend to have all the answers to the complex and vitally important work of educating students who have experienced trauma. The ideas, examples, resources, tools, and stories we share are part of a larger research base and a larger conversation about trauma-sensitive practices. But we believe there's value in contributing our firsthand accounts, both of what comes of trusting in students when they've lost trust in themselves and the positive results members of a school staff can achieve when they risk being vulnerable and authentic with one another.

Here is what's waiting for you in the pages ahead:

- **Chapter 1** unearths common biases and barriers that prevent students, teachers, and school leaders from engaging in practices that support learners affected by trauma.
- **Chapter 2** shows you and your staff ways to design all-school events and daily lesson plans to reduce the risk that they will retraumatize vulnerable students.
- **Chapter 3** takes an honest look at the discipline practices that often perpetuate the very problems they're intended to address.
- **Chapter 4** looks at ways you might design, or redesign, the physical spaces in your school to foster a more trauma-sensitive culture and climate.
- **Chapter 5** takes on a topic that often presents a challenge for students, teachers, and school leaders: being vulnerable enough to ask for help.

- **Chapter 6** provides an in-depth look at developing relationships with traumatized students and giving them the tools they need for self-care.
- **Chapter 7** focuses on a sometimes-overlooked aspect of working with students who have experienced or are experiencing trauma: secondary trauma, experienced by teachers and other staff members.
- **Chapter 8** closes the book with a call to action: giving students hope for, and faith in, their future and their success.

Several of the forms in this book are available for download at **www.ascd.org/trauma-sensitive-school-leadership.** Look for a download icon next to figures.

As you read, we urge you to reflect on the content as it applies to you as an educator and school leader and to the practices and culture at your school. To that end, each chapter closes with a collection of self-reflection prompts designed to help you connect what you've read to the reality of your school, your staff, and your students. Because the social-emotional well-being of students is everyone's responsibility, and because educating students who are living with trauma is a job best undertaken as a team, we recommend gathering with members of your school leadership team to share and discuss your reflections and plan your next steps forward.

Trauma-sensitive education has life-changing implications for the children in your care. As you read, we urge you to remember the faith, hope, and love that can be both built and expressed through teaching, learning, and leading . . . and that your efforts as educator will ripple through the lives of students for decades to come.

1

Biases and Barriers

Factors That Prevent Schools from Addressing Trauma

The giant computer that is our unconscious silently crunches all the data it can from the experiences we've had, the people we've met, the lessons we've learned, the books we've read, the movies we've seen, and so on, and it forms an opinion.

———————————

—Malcolm Gladwell—
Blink: The Power of Thinking Without Thinking

To help all students thrive, school administrators must first address the biases and barriers that prevent educators from providing students suffering from trauma with the support they need. In this chapter, we will explore two types of bias—*implicit* and *explicit*—and the importance of maintaining a continual focus on equity.

Let's begin with a hard truth: the past and present trauma students carry with them is too often viewed as a weakness, with educators thinking that the best way forward is to "toughen kids up" so that they will be better equipped to "fight back" against the trauma that is holding them back. Beliefs like this feed into a narrative that encourages educators to underplay the reality of trauma, devalue those who experience it, assign false motivation to these students' behavior, and unknowingly punish students for behaviors that are beyond their control.

One of the first steps in addressing trauma is simply acknowledging its existence and lasting impact. It means ceasing to pretend that life is always painless, that childhood is happy and carefree, and that "most" kids easily bounce back from difficult experiences. Educators succeed by creating an authentic and honest connection with students, and it's not possible to do this without understanding that trauma is common in student populations, comes from various sources, and manifests in many ways.

Dr. Nadine Burke-Harris, the surgeon general of California, has discussed the influence of trauma on school-age children, noting that many students experience

> things like physical abuse, emotional abuse, sexual abuse, physical and emotional neglect, parental mental illness, parental substance dependence, parental incarceration, and parental separation or divorce. Those are the adverse childhood experiences criteria, or the ACEs criteria, that we . . . have been tracking. (California School Boards Association, 2013, para. 2)

Biases as Barriers

Everyone has biases. Some biases develop over time and occur without malice. Having biases does not make you a bad person; it's part of *being* a person. All people are shaped for better or for worse by life experiences.

Recognizing that it is human nature to have biases enables honest examination of them, including how both hidden and overt biases can present a barrier to reaching students who have experienced trauma. Sometimes educators live in their own little bubbles and only see things through their own worldview. This approach doesn't encourage them to make the effort and take the time to look at things from a completely different perspective: that of students who often live different lives than their teachers do.

When Andrea was a relatively new teacher, her school district encouraged every staff member to ride two afternoon bus routes sometime during the school year. Andrea picked a couple of students she did not know very much about and rode their buses. It was an eye-opening experience for her and ultimately led to a total shift in how she handled things in her classroom—everything from routines to discipline and homework assignments. How she wished she had ridden those bus routes during her first year of teaching!

During the bus rides, Andrea sat toward the middle of the bus and could hear conversations in both directions. The older students were talking about things and using language that struck her as very inappropriate given the younger students sitting all around them. It made her wonder about the things they were hearing and seeing on a daily basis, and it made her concerned about their younger siblings.

As her students were getting off their bus, a few turned around and waved proudly at Andrea; they were happy that she knew where they lived, seeing it as a new connection. Others did not wave and probably wished she had not seen their homes. She saw families waiting for students at the door or on the porch to greet them after their day of learning. She saw parts of the community that she had never seen and some she will never be able to forget. The bus rides made Andrea realize more than ever that some of her students came to school to learn and some came to escape their current reality. Educators need to meet students where they are in order to really help them achieve.

Racial Bias

To understand the racial bias that affects many in the United States, all you need to do is to watch the evening news. But racial bias isn't kept outside the schoolhouse doors—just the opposite. As Madeleine Will observes in *EdWeek,* "Teachers are just as likely to have racial biases as nonteachers" (2020, para. 1). This finding emerged from a study conducted by Starck and colleagues (2020), which examined the pro-white explicit and implicit racial biases held by teachers and nonteachers and found only negligible differences between the populations. If the goal is to confront and address the effects of systemic and pervasive racism, everyone working in education needs to realize the role they play in perpetuating racial inequality in schools. If education is to effectively promote racial equity, school leaders must provide training that either shifts or mitigates the effects of their own and teachers' racial biases.

Racial bias by educators is harming students and preventing them from experiencing a full educational experience similar to that of their peers (Dhaliwal, 2020; Gershenson & Papageorge, 2021). And racial bias in education settings can definitely be traumatic for students. Carter (2007) puts it plainly:

Traumatic events that occur as a result of witnessing or experiencing racism, discrimination, or structural prejudice (also known as institutional racism) can have a profound impact on the mental health of individuals exposed to these events. Racial trauma (also known as *race-based traumatic stress*) refers to the stressful impact or emotional pain of one's experience with racism and discrimination. (Edwards, 2020, para. 25)

When Justin was in middle school, all students were required to take shop class. He had never been good with using tools, so he was not particularly comfortable there. The teacher was popular and well respected—someone a lot of students looked up to—and also had a habit of teasing guys in the class, especially those who could not hammer and cut wood as well as he thought a boy should. One day Justin and his friends were talking about one of their favorite topics at the time (girls), and the teacher overheard them. The teacher told Justin he'd never have a chance with the girl he had mentioned. At first, the boys laughed, thinking their teacher was just joking around in the way they were used to, until he added, "They don't match." Everyone got quiet, realizing the teacher was referring to the fact that Justin was Black and the young lady he was talking about was not. It was an awkward moment. The teacher seemed to realize that he had crossed a line. He kept Justin after class and explained earnestly that he had meant no offense. He was only trying to help. After all, the girl's family probably would not like the idea of her dating Justin. And just when Justin thought things couldn't get worse, the teacher began suggesting "alternatives"—other girls at school whom Justin might pursue instead. All the girls he mentioned were Black.

Although it's clear now that it was the teacher who was out of line, Justin was incredibly embarrassed by the incident. His buddies who had witnessed it teased him about it, as did others in the school when they heard about it later. He found himself newly anxious about going to school, and he positively dreaded going to shop, so much that it affected his ability to concentrate in the math class he had prior to it. The shop teacher had never actively discriminated against Justin; he was always willing to help him and treated him no differently than any other students in the class. Yet in sharing his very biased views on who should date whom, he had unintentionally created a traumatic experience for a 12-year-old Black male who already struggled with issues of race in a predominantly white school. This incident is one of the reasons that today, as a school counselor influencing many young minds, Justin actively self-examines what he says and does to keep his own biases in check.

We share this story to drive home the point that *words*—what is said, how it is said, and to whom it is said—can have a tremendous effect on students, every day, in school. Educators are human; everyone has some type of bias. What happened to Justin can happen to other students when teachers don't make a regular practice of checking their biases and examining their words and actions. Figure 1.1 highlights a number of key areas for reflection.

The process of reflecting on racial bias at your school is the first step toward equity. Talk to your students of color. Get their perspectives on learning in your school (see the section on gathering student feedback in Chapter 6). What racial biases do they perceive in your school? Be courageous enough to ask the difficult questions, challenge the status quo, and—this is key—take action to dismantle institutional racism. This might mean increasing the number of minority students enrolled in your AP and honors courses. It might mean encouraging a more diverse group of students to consider dual enrollment courses that not only boost their confidence in academic ability, but also build a foundation for continued learning in a postsecondary setting. As you consider the prompts in Figure 1.1, make some notes about what actions might be appropriate for your school.

1.1 Reflection on Racial Bias

Instructions: Examine your school's data for each focus area and reflect on your response.			
Focus Areas	**No**	**Getting There**	**Yes**
Does enrollment in your higher academic courses (e.g., honors, AP, IB) reflect your school's demographics?			
Is there an even distribution of awards/accolades/celebrations that reflects the demographics of your classes and school?			
Does discipline reflect the demographics in your school? For example, is there an even distribution of discipline?			
Do the number of students participating in extracurricular activities reflect the demographics of your school?			
Do the number of students' academic honors reflect the demographics in your classes and school?			
Is there an equitable number of students that score Advanced on standardized testing in your school?			
Do drop-out rates reflect the demographics of your school?			
Notes for Further Action			

"Color Blindness"

"I don't see color" is something that many people have said as a way to convey that they do not hold racial biases and should not be perceived as racist. But valuing "color blindness" is a barrier in itself—one that perpetuates the privilege that many white people have experienced throughout their lives. "Not seeing color" denies the lived experiences of other people and denies systemic racism (Vincenty, 2020). In addition, it undercuts and undervalues the racial identity of students (Ferlazzo, 2019). In an article for AASA, Beverly Daniel Tatum, author of the 2017 book *Why Are All the Black Kids Sitting Together in the Cafeteria?*, acknowledged both the good intentions color blindness can reflect as well as the damage it can do:

> Many teachers aspire to be "color-blind" when interacting with their students. To notice the racial and ethnic differences among their students feels wrong to them, a sign perhaps of bigotry or prejudicial thinking. But from the child's point of view (and that of his or her parents), not noticing may mean that the educator is overlooking an important dimension of the young person's experience in the world and, even more specifically, in that classroom. A color-blind approach often means that the educator has not considered the meaning of racial/ethnic identity to the child. (n.d., para. 2)

It is impossible to look at someone and not see their skin color. When educators say they don't see color, students hear that their rich culture, traditions, and the foundation of who they are as people are not important. When teachers "don't see color," it allows them to turn a blind eye to the issues and disparities that affect people of color. Bias runs contrary to the conscious mind, and the only way to overcome it is to face it head-on and make a conscious decision to move past it.

Misunderstanding of Trauma

Someone who didn't grow up experiencing significant trauma might consider "trauma" to be a temporary setback or a roadblock in the path of progress rather than what it is: a potentially lifelong struggle to climb what can seem to be an insurmountable mountain.

Educators who didn't experience trauma or witness its effects on someone close to them can be quick to judge a student for struggling even years after the traumatic experience. For example, an educator who grew up in a loving, two-parent household might not accurately measure the negative effect divorce can have on a student's academic achievement, social and emotional well-being, and life. Not understanding trauma's effect on students can prevent teachers from providing useful interventions.

The guided reflection in Figure 1.2 provides a list of phrases that suggest an educator may have an unawareness of or a bias against appreciating the effects of trauma. Statements such as these minimize, ignore, or disregard trauma. This kind of talk only hurts kids

1.2 Reflection on Trauma Bias: Staff Comments to Students

Statement	I've heard this a lot	I've heard this once or twice	Our staff would never say this
Instructions: Reflect on the frequency of each statement's occurrence at your school.			
Life's not fair.			
Get over it.			
Stop acting like a child/baby.			
Stop letting that bother you.			
Grow up.			
Toughen up.			
Keep that to yourself.			
It's time you moved beyond this.			
Act your age.			
What is wrong with you?			
Calm down!			
Notes for Further Action			

and will cause them to pull away from educators and become disconnected from their school.

Racial bias, "color blindness," and misunderstanding of trauma are all barriers that prevent school administrators from addressing trauma in their schools. Only by identifying these barriers and determining how they may be holding you back and ways you can break free of them can you truly address the trauma that exists in your school, with both students and staff.

Let's move on to positive actions you can take.

▶ Accept the Reality and Ubiquity of Trauma

One of the first things you can do to advance equity and access for all your students is to promote a simple, yet profound, mindset shift. When faced with a student who is struggling academically, acting out, shutting down, confronting, retreating, inattentive, fixated, or displaying other behaviors considered undesirable for the classroom or school, before thinking (or asking), "What's wrong with you?" take a breath and think (or ask), "What happened to you?"

When you think about it, "What's wrong with you?" is a question that's not really a question. It's a statement of judgment, immediately identifying "you" as defective, flawed, hostile, discardable. "What happened to you?" is something quite different. It acknowledges the whole, complicated person and is a first step in restoring and renewing the beauty and purpose that this person represents.

This may be a new way for you and your teachers to view trauma. Certainly trauma can display itself in very overt, in-your-face behaviors and responses, but it can also be silent or present itself in hidden ways—even via hypertension, diabetes, and other physical maladies that manifest decades after the initial traumatic events took place (Felitti et al., 1999).

Before going any further into the work of improving school so that it "works better" for more learners, remember that trauma has been a part of life for many children and adults. Also remember that your goal is to create and nurture learning spaces and experiences that will help students find success beyond their past history. They deserve your attention and your intervention. One of the beautiful things about doing this work is realizing that many changes you can implement to support students who have experienced trauma will also help many other students who do not have the same history of traumatic events. Your actions—both what you choose to do and purposefully choose *not* to do—can help create a learning community where all learners have the opportunity to thrive and excel.

An administrator-led, schoolwide shift toward *What happened to you?* thinking is powerful because it helps break down some of the most common biases about children with trauma. As we explore the role of bias, we encourage you to read and reflect with an eye on your own beliefs and biases. Everyone brings a lens to the conversation; realizing exactly what your lens favors—or discards—can be a powerful beginning to the important work of educating a student population with a rising number of mental health concerns. As Leeb and colleagues (2020) note, "Compared with 2019, the proportion of mental health– related visits for children aged 5–11 and 12–17 years increased approximately 24 percent and 31 percent, respectively" (para. 2).

Have you ever overheard comments like these from teachers— or caught yourself thinking these kinds of thoughts?

- "This kid has got to stop crying at school."
- "The way he refuses to answer me just shows how disrespectful he is."
- "She argues about everything! I'll show her that I always win in the end."

- "If they'd just go to bed at a more reasonable hour, they could stay awake in class."

Trauma lingers. It's not something a child can simply forget about and get over. It's not a cold that comes, causes the sniffles, and then leaves. Trauma is often carried throughout one's life, and its effects can surface unbidden and in response to all kinds of triggers. That student always on the verge of tears may be thinking of a parent or sibling they have lost. The student who won't respond may be living in a home where a raised voice or direct confrontation means violence is imminent and silence is the safest bet.

Similarly, a power struggle with an argumentative student could reflect that argument is the only effective way this student has found to keep herself feeling safe and powerful. A sleeping student may feel so responsible and value education so much that they try to complete their coursework after taking care of three younger siblings every afternoon and evening. Or—after reading, cooking, bathing, putting them to bed, and housecleaning—they are exhausted and can neither concentrate nor complete their homework. The teacher's voice in class can become a potent sleep aid for such a student.

▶ Accept Responsibility for Responding to Trauma

Instead of expecting a student serving as "proxy parent" to just "figure it out" and find a way to turn in homework on time, or expecting a student who recently lost a home or a family member to "get over it and move on," we educators need to shift those "figure it out" and "get over it" expectations to ourselves. As adults, it's we who have the greater capacity to do both; as professionals, it's our obligation.

So, for example, step back and consider why homework is worth so much in your teachers' gradebooks. Meet with teachers and brainstorm three new ways to allow students to show what they know. Encourage everyone to work on "getting over" feeling hurt, threatened, or embarrassed when students act out or talk back, and focus instead on finding positive responses when even their most well-intended decisions are met with disdain and resistance. A student's legitimate trauma is not something that can be resolved with a change in attitude. An adult staff member, teacher, or administrator's frustration, on the other hand, can be mitigated with understanding and with effective strategies.

It's important to stress that accepting responsibility for responding to trauma is on all adults in the school—not just the school counselor or counselors! Of course, if you are fortunate enough to have dedicated school counselors, you probably also know that they have multiple duties and responsibilities. Dealing and working with students who are suffering is a job best managed through a team approach. We say this fully recognizing the demands and constraints of educators' schedules can be a barrier to teacher–counselor collaboration. It is incumbent upon you, as a school leader, to lead your staff through this barrier—to find ways, or a system, to keep key stakeholders in the loop when students are struggling with the effects of trauma. Child Find conversations, intervention teams, and short report-outs during faculty meetings all can help keep this work collaborative and at the forefront of the culture. Updates from teachers about student check-ins can also help; we talk about this more in Chapter 6.

When all staff members are willing to embrace being trauma-sensitive, it supports the counseling team's role and provides additional support for students in their learning.

The time to act is now. If you wait until all the conditions are perfect or until you're sure you know exactly what to do, you will never begin. Remember, "anything worth doing is worth doing poorly at first." This is not a call to mediocrity but a call to action.

Connect with your colleagues, listen to your students and community, and decide where you will act first. You only steward the education of your students for a short time. Are you continuously working to create the best conditions possible for every student's success? Bear in mind Andratesha Fritzgerald's warning that "inaction is agreement. Inaction is racism. Inaction is injustice. Inaction is inhumane. Inaction is not an option" (2020, p. 12).

▶ Dedicate Yourself to Continuous Improvement

Although it's more than fine to get started with a novice's skill level, you don't want to stay there. Part of the commitment to action is to take action; the next part is to keep getting better at it.

When the strategies, systems, interventions, and practices you build become the embedded habits and norms of your school, then you're getting good at it. When trauma-informed practices stop being an "event" and become "the way we do school," then you are setting up a space and an environment where kids will find success. This includes academic achievement, but also personal growth, enhanced social-emotional skills, and improved well-being in all aspects of their lives. You need practice to get good at caring for students, accepting them 100 percent as they are when they arrive in your school.

Figure 1.3 presents different levels of understanding trauma-informed instructional practice and learning. Where do you stand in terms of being trauma-informed? What do you know about

1.3 Trauma-Informed Learning: Levels of Understanding and Interest

CLUELESS
I don't know anything about trauma-informed learning

SKILLED
I lead others in learning about trauma-informed learning

NOT INTERESTED
I don't feel like I need to know about trauma-informed learning

APPLYING
I am practicing trauma-informed learning in my teaching

NOVICE
I don't know much, but I am eager to learn and grow

LEARNING
I am currently learning about trauma-informed learning

establishing a climate of trauma-informed learning? Do you feel ready and equipped to tackle the challenges of educating students affected by trauma? Be patient. It doesn't happen overnight; it's a journey that strengthens with time.

Making improvements requires taking an honest look at existing perceptions and actions. What are you doing right? What can you do better? Can you envision where you want to be?

▶ Be Real and Authentic

No person lives the carefree, happy-all-the-time, problem-free life often portrayed in television shows and movies. Social media posts many times also present this rosy view: only one's very best moments are selfie-worthy (and there seems to be a lot of them). It can be easy to believe that the selective, best-foot-forward media stream is actually someone's life.

Getting past this deception is essential to helping students. Students need to develop a critical eye toward happy-all-the-time posts—and you and your staff can model authentic lives for them, while living and learning together at school. Bill and Dave often remind each other that staff members don't want perfect leaders (who don't exist anyway); they want authentic leaders. Your students don't want perfect teachers and perfect classrooms; they want authentic experiences. You honor them when you present your real self. This doesn't mean snapping at students in anger, but instead letting them know the day started with an experience that caused some frustration. A statement like "I want you to know I may be a little impatient today. Please let me know if I'm not being respectful or I don't sound like myself during class" shares one's authentic self while modeling honesty for students. We'll talk more about sharing our stories in Chapter 5.

▶ Maintain a Safe Place for Students

An educator's role is to assist students not just in their academic growth but also in their quest to become caring, decent people. Students who come from homes where they are called stupid or constantly put down certainly do not need to get that same message from their teachers.

Many students do come to school for an escape. Sometimes a student just wants to feel safe for a few hours every day. Many of them come to school looking for hope. That hope can come in the form of positive attention or feedback from an adult. For other students, the school breakfast and lunch may be the only meals they are certain they will receive on a given day.

All students deserve to have educators in their lives who are empathetic and understanding. Consider your own life. How many times have you had to deal with going to work and teaching with a heavy heart, or reacting negatively to someone because baggage from your personal life is weighing you down?

Trauma is real. As we mentioned earlier in this chapter, responding to its effects requires more than simply sending students to the school counselor or school psychologist. The days of writing hall passes and sending students to Guidance and hoping they come back fixed are long past. Increasing trends in suicide attempts, depression, anxiety attacks, and other mental health concerns (Leeb et al., 2020) may require professional resources beyond those in your school building. You also need to build, at your school, a cohesive, collaborative group of professionals with a better understanding of how trauma affects all facets of educating students. Building better relationships with students positively influences both their academic performance and their social-emotional well-being.

▶ Focus on the Whole Child

Way too often, school leaders are focused solely on academic achievement. They base success and failure on test scores or comparing their school's data to that of other schools. This mindset is a fatal trap that prevents implementing a well-rounded focus on the social-emotional wellness of students, which is the essence of trauma-informed leadership that truly supports students. What good are high test scores if a child is contemplating suicide? As the four of us look back on our educational experiences as kids, we don't remember the facts and figures our teachers taught us;

we remember how they made us feel, if they believed in us, and if they cared about us. The same is true today. Ten years from now at a class reunion, students won't be talking about how that one teacher helped them pass that standardized exam; they will be talking about the teacher who was there for them when their dad died, the principal who grieved with them when their house burned to the ground, the school counselor who offered support and reassurance when their parents split up. Put aside the focus on testing and focus on what is important: kids.

Figure 1.4 illustrates how three different areas of school leadership—a focus on trauma-informed practice, on SEL and student well-being, and on academic achievement—can come together to serve the whole child.

1.4 School Leadership That Focuses on The Whole Child

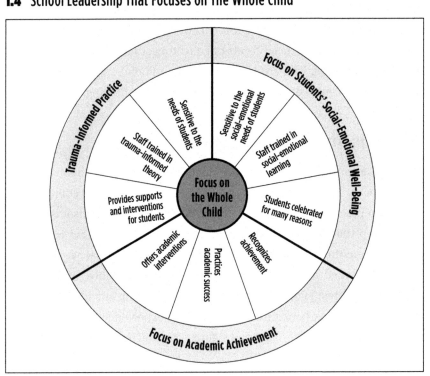

▶ Educate Yourself About Adverse Childhood Experiences

Recent research and writing on adverse childhood experiences (ACEs) have shined a light on just how important it is for educators to consider the ways in which students' experiences outside school can affect learning and behavior. ACEs are stressful life events that occur during the first 18 years of a child's life. They include natural disasters, death in the family, poverty, and racism, as well as experiences of abuse and neglect, and exposure to domestic violence and other forms of household dysfunction, including separation and divorce, psychopathology, and parental incarceration (Trossman et al., 2021). Educators must understand that these stressors and traumatic experiences physically alter the development of students' brains, which, in turn, affects everything from their capacity to learn to their ability to form relationships (Filetti et al., 1999).

It stands to reason that there are children in every classroom who have experienced some level of trauma. It is inevitable that the trauma that directly affects students' lives and their abilities in the classroom trickles down to those who work with these students on a daily basis. It is time to equip educators so they can better support students who have experienced trauma. Trauma affects adults, too. Some of your teachers may have lingering trauma from their own childhoods, whereas others may be experiencing secondary trauma as they absorb some of the pain and stress they are helping students manage and overcome.

👥 Reflecting on Biases and Barriers

Overcoming the biases and barriers that prevent a school from adequately serving students affected by trauma is everyone's job, but it's your responsibility to lead the way.

- Review your responses to Figure 1.1 and Figure 1.2. What challenges do you face in your school? Where does your team need to grow?
- What blind spots or biases are preventing you and your team from adequately supporting students affected by trauma?
- What challenged your thinking the most in this chapter?

Meet with the members of your school leadership team to share and discuss your reflections and plan your next steps forward.

2

Do No Harm

Taking Steps to Avoid Retraumatizing Students

Our human compassion binds us the one to the other—not in pity or patronisingly, but as human beings who have learnt how to turn our common suffering into hope for the future.

—Nelson Mandela—
"The Healing of Our Land," Johannesburg, 2000

Sometimes the best-intended actions and comments can trigger traumatic memories and painful emotional responses.

For example, no one would argue that school safety is a key concern for school leaders. Most of us acknowledge the importance of holding fire drills, bus evacuation drills, and active-shooter drills.

But it's equally clear how these drills could be traumatic, both in themselves and in their power to evoke past frightening or negative experiences with guns, fire, car accidents, or even hiding from someone who you fear might do you harm. We aren't saying that school leaders don't need to—and should not—practice school safety drills. But we are saying it's beneficial to use the lens of trauma to consider how these drills may affect the people in your building and take steps to mitigate the harm.

Situations that should be viewed through this lens don't need to be as emotionally heavy as an active-shooter drill. Just the sound of a teacher shouting at a hallway of disruptive students can trigger a physical, neurological, and emotional response for someone who has been emotionally, sexually, or physically abused. And the devastating truth is that there is a very good chance that many people within your building—both students and staff—are vulnerable to this kind of triggering. Consider that Felitti and colleagues' (1999) study of adverse childhood experiences found that 52 percent of adults taking the survey had experienced one or more types of neglect, trauma, or home-based challenges the researchers asked about.

The Harm We Can Do

For many years, corporal punishment was both a common practice in U.S. schools and a largely unexamined one. Justin vividly remembers a paddle that his elementary school principal used. Students were terrified of that paddle and of that principal. In theory, the point of corporal punishment (which is still legal in 19 U.S. states) is consequence-based deterrence. But what benefit does corporal punishment provide, other than permeating a sense of fear and intimidation?

Children have always been affected by traumas occurring in their lives; it's appalling to think that some still consider corporal punishment to be an acceptable response to unacceptable behaviors. Think about the students you encounter who have had some really traumatizing circumstances in their lives; what effect would physical punishment have on them?

Educators don't often reflect on their work in the light of "Am I causing harm to anyone in my class or school?" but doing so is a way to prevent retraumatizing students at school. As a school leader, you must be willing to unearth systemic issues in your school—things like maintaining homogeneous grouping, lack of sensitivity to cultural differences, and unspoken beliefs about who can learn and who cannot—that hold students back, hindering their growth or resurfacing trauma they have experienced at home.

According to Paul Gorski, founder of the Equity Literacy Institute and EdChange, "true trauma-informed work . . . must recognize and address the *school's* role in creating or re-creating trauma. In fact, that should be the starting point" (Gaffney, 2019, para. 15). It seems obvious, but we will say it anyway: kids can't afford to be retraumatized, especially in school, which should be a safe haven where they feel safe, confident, protected, and welcomed. School leaders must intentionally focus on and be willing to revise common practices, policies, and procedures within the school.

Many of the things that educators are doing that retraumatize kids, such as regaining control of class by shouting, giving a zero for late work instead of asking why it was late, or correcting a single student's action in front of the class to make a point, have been handed down for generations. Some teachers still think these antiquated practices are right and necessary. In this chapter, we review some terms and foundational principles, spotlight practices that need reconsideration, and suggest concrete ways to nurture a school culture that bolsters the learning of students affected by trauma.

Simple Versus Complex Trauma

Trauma can be simple or complex. *Simple traumas* are experiences that happened within a given time frame (e.g., car accident, injury) that produced an intense reaction and emotional suffering. A death, a divorce or separation—these brief simple traumas can be very painful. *Complex trauma* involves repeated, ongoing exposure to traumatic experiences. This could be going home daily to a neighborhood that is not safe, or to parents who are abusive toward each other; it is repeated trauma that is, for the person experiencing it, hard to escape.

According to the National Child Traumatic Stress Network (n.d.), complex trauma encompasses both children's exposure to multiple traumatic events—often of an invasive, interpersonal nature—and the wide-ranging, long-term effects of this exposure. These events are severe and pervasive, such as abuse or profound neglect. They usually occur early in life and can disrupt many aspects of a child's development and the formation of a sense of self. Because these events often occur with a caregiver, they interfere with the child's ability to form a secure attachment. Many aspects of healthy physical and mental development rely on a primary source of safety and stability.

Close to 40 percent of students in the U.S. have been exposed to some form of traumatic stressor affecting their current and future lives, with sexual assault, physical assault, and witnessing domestic violence being the most prevalent (California School Boards Association, 2013; Felitti et al., 1999). For an overview of the various forms that trauma can take, see Figure 2.1.

2.1 An Overview of Adverse Childhood Experiences

Category	Examples
Abuse	• *Emotional abuse:* A parent, stepparent, or adult living in your home swore at you, insulted you, put you down, or acted in a way that made you afraid that you might be physically hurt. • *Physical abuse:* A parent, stepparent, or adult living in your home pushed, grabbed, slapped, threw something at you, or hit you so hard that you had marks or were injured. • Sexual abuse: An adult, relative, family friend, or stranger who was at least five years older than you touched or fondled your body in a sexual way, made you touch his/her body in a sexual way, or attempted to have any type of sexual intercourse with you.
Household challenges	• *Family guardian treated violently:* Your parent or other guardian was pushed, grabbed, or slapped; had something thrown at them; was kicked, bitten, hit with a fist, hit with something hard, repeatedly hit for at least a few minutes, or ever threatened or hurt by a knife or gun by their partner or significant other. • *Substance abuse:* A household member was a problem drinker or alcoholic, or a household member used street drugs. • *Mental illness:* A household member was depressed or mentally ill or a household member attempted suicide. • *Parental separation or divorce:* Your parents were ever separated or divorced. • *Incarceration:* A household member went to prison.
Neglect	• *Emotional neglect:* Someone in your family made you feel unimportant or unwanted, you felt unloved, people in your family didn't look out for each other or feel close to each other, or your family was a source of worry and anxiety. • *Physical neglect:* There was no one to take care of you, protect you, or take you to the doctor if you needed it; you didn't have enough to eat; or your parents were too drunk or too high to take care of you, and you had to wear dirty clothes.

Source: Felitti et al., 1999.

▶ Use a Trauma-Informed Lens to Examine School Practices

Honest and purposeful reflection is essential to your work as a school leader. This introspection into what you do, why and how you do it, and who you are helps you to grow and improve.

All educators have had moments or situations in their careers that they wish they had done differently. Have you ever lost it and yelled at a kid who was really getting to you? Although there are times when raising your voice might be appropriate (e.g., to emphasize a point in the context of a certain story, to catch someone's attention in time to prevent an accident), that's different from shouting in frustration and anger. Doing so destroys the safe haven—the break from fighting, arguing, and the combat zone "home" may represent—for some students. As noted, for too many students, home is not a safe space. Being at school is an escape for many students from abuse, both verbal and physical, from their caregivers. For some of your students, yelling and screaming is the main form of communication and resolution of problems at home. This traumatic experience leaves scars.

Reflective introspection about your practice as a school leader and educator requires some hard and honest conversations—ones that can and should lead you to identify systemic issues and revise practices that might be hurting or triggering kids. We will look closely at both the issues and the necessary action steps. For example, are you exclusively using homogeneous grouping in your school? We will examine that in Chapter 4. Are you, perhaps unconsciously, holding on to certain ideas about who can and cannot learn? We'll look at that in Chapter 5. Are you not as sensitive as you might be to cultural differences? This will be the focus of Chapter 6.

One tool we recommend for the work of identifying and ending damaging practices is the acronym HARM. When reviewing your current approaches and when planning new initiatives and events, consider the following points:

- **H**ow would someone who has experienced abuse or neglect react to this lesson, question, or experience?

- **A**re students with household challenges likely to experience a retriggering of their trauma?
- **R**econsider the planned lesson, drill, or event through a lens of emotional or physical neglect your students may bring.
- **M**ental illness is common; are you supporting understanding and awareness?

Every conversation, lesson, small-group activity, or school-wide event includes students who have been negatively influenced by trauma. What is the tone of teachers in the classrooms in your school? Are they sarcastic? Do they raise their voices? Every educator in your school should carefully select the words, tone, actions, and approach used in working with students.

▶ Make Safety Drills Feel Safer

Safety drills have long been a part of school life. Fire drills are familiar to everyone. Depending on where you live, you may have experienced tornado drills. Depending on when you went to school, you may have been taught in school how to brace for bomb attacks or what to do if there is an active shooter in the building. Educators may wish there was no need to bring these kinds of stressful and triggering events into school, but they are a responsibility we must carry out. Figure 2.2 provides four keys to making safety drills feel safer and less traumatizing.

The bottom line? Don't surprise students and staff with safety drills that could trigger and resurface trauma. That's right: we said students *and staff.* The effects of trauma do not magically disappear in adulthood, and there will absolutely be staff members in your school who will benefit from advance notification of potentially stressful events and follow-up support.

2.2 Four Keys to Safer Safety Drills

1. Include school counselors in planning every drill.
Touch base with your school counselor before running any safety drills to see if there are any students who might need additional support or should be exempted from participating in the drill.

2. Announce all drills in advance.
Announcing safety drills provide forewarning to students and adults in the school who have experienced trauma. It allows them to arrange for accommodations, opt out, or connect with a school counselor.

3. Identify a safe space.
Provide students who have experienced trauma a safe place in the building or another building where they can go to not be engaged in the drill. The setback that a safety drill could cause a student is not worth the benefits that you think will come from the drill.

4. Ensure support is available.
Have empathetic adult staff (e.g., school counselors, other personnel prepared for the role) and trained peer counselors standing by to reassure students who have experienced trauma that they are safe.

The National Child Traumatic Stress Network (2018) also has recommended strategic steps to support students during school safety drills, including teaching students

> coping strategies such as breathing techniques or [identifying] buddy students to accompany them during the drill. Identify any potential trauma or loss reminders that may trigger students and adapt the plan accordingly. (p. 2)

Say, for example, that your school had a recent emergency during which the fire alarm was used. When it's time for the next fire drill, instead of using the fire alarm, consider announcing the evacuation order over the public address system.

Remember, too, that opting out can be an option! It's easy to fall in the trap of requiring everyone to participate in all events that take place in a school. But certain activities—including safety drills but also videos, stories, or illustrations shared in assemblies—might trigger a student or a staff member's traumatic experience. Stay informed, and don't hesitate to prioritize individual well-being over 100 percent participation.

▶ Get All Staff on Board

All educators need a basic sense of trauma-informed practice. They need to be aware that there are students all around them who have been affected in some way by abuse, household challenges, and neglect, and they need to remember that they may never know *which* students are carrying these burdens. That's why it's important for all staff in your building to do the following:

- **Treat all students as if they were affected by trauma.** Doing so creates a trauma-sensitive and trauma-informed setting that builds others up and respects their life journey.
- **Stay calm, positive, encouraging, nurturing, and supportive.** Classrooms where these principles reign allow students to thrive beyond the trauma that they have encountered.
- **Track individual behavioral triggers**. Teachers may not know the why behind a student's reaction or the feelings a particular trigger evokes, but they can track the trigger points to help the student feel more comfortable in the classroom. For example, if a student stutters, clams up, or begins to cry when someone is raising their voice in the classroom, the teacher can mark this down as an observable trigger that causes a reaction from the student to try and reduce this type of behavior in the classroom. Stories or videos that feature violence or other plot points or character actions that most students find

unremarkable can also be triggering. Unannounced emergency drills are another common trigger that can quickly drag a student back to the trauma they experienced. By tracking and keeping data on triggers, the teacher and support staff can better mitigate them and help keep students from being retraumatized in the classroom.

- **Learn and use the HARM acronym to regularly reflect their own practices.** These questions are valuable for content teams designing lessons, teachers delivering instruction and planning activities, cafeteria staff who serve meals and monitor student interactions, coaches, office staff . . . the list goes on.

Figure 2.3 shows three things you can and should do to build staff awareness of trauma.

2.3 Three Ways to Build Your Staff's Trauma Sensitivity

1. Provide trauma-informed professional learning.
Design learning for your staff with the understanding that there will be students throughout the school who are affected by trauma. Teach teachers to identify potentially triggering content and to redesign lessons in a more trauma-informed way. The strategies discussed in Chapter 6 are a great start. Focusing on mindfulness, building on-ramps, giving students choice in assignments and assessments, and coteaching with counselors are all worthy topics for all-staff professional learning.

2. Provide follow-up.
Check in with your staff after trauma-sensitivity training to see how they are doing and if they have further questions or concerns. Ask them if they would like to connect with a counselor who can provide them with additional guidance.

3. Be an example.
Model what you want to see in the classroom in your own leadership practices. Use meetings, communications, and professional training sessions to illustrate the kinds of interventions, adjustments, and advance trigger notifications you want to see throughout your school.

▶ Encourage Teachers to Differentiate Instruction

Far too often, teachers assign one assignment, one piece of home-work, or one assessment. This arrangement may be easier on the teacher, but it will almost certainly present difficulties for some students.

Differentiated instruction frees a student to choose or *not* choose content that could trigger their trauma and set them back. It also allows them to learn in ways that they are ready to embrace. For example, a student may choose to work independently if they feel unready to be in a group setting. In this way, differentiated instruction returns power to the individual student, giving them free-dom and choice to take control of the situation rather than having someone control them. Especially when it's conducted with flexible grouping that varies how students work, what they work on, and with whom they work, differentiated instruction is a way for teachers to remove as many barriers to student learning and self-expression as possible. It gives them more avenues for choice and customization, more opportunities to feel successful and engaged, and more oppor-tunities to trust. Something as seemingly simple as encouraging stu-dents to choose the assignment that most appeals to them from a range of assignment options can be confidence boosting.

Teacher Katie Usher (2019) emphasizes the importance of dif-ferentiation and offering choices:

> When I give my students a choice on how they'll complete a proj-ect, they have to meet certain criteria, but I allow them to find an outlet they find most enjoyable. . . . Giving students a choice allows them to take ownership of their learning as well as create a prod-uct that feels authentic to them. They work on something that they're good at creating, or try something they want to get better at. (para. 3)

Giving students ownership over choice empowers them to become productive and responsible adults who are able to make decisions with confidence. Mike Anderson, in *Learning to Choose, Choosing to Learn* (2016), has noted that choice

> can help students self-differentiate their learning so work is more appropriately challenging. [It may] also combat student apathy, helping students connect with their strengths and interests and giving them more autonomy, power, and control over their work, which boosts their intrinsic motivation. These are perhaps the two most compelling reasons to use choice as a part of daily teaching and learning in schools, but there are . . . other additional benefits. . . . Students engage in deeper, richer learning. Students display more on-task behavior. Students' social and emotional learning increases. The learning environment becomes more collaborative. (p. 17)

▶ Respect Student Silence

It's common for educators to ask questions, prod, or encourage students to share their stories of struggle. They may be curious about what happened, be looking for insight that will help them provide more effective support, or just believe it's better to "talk things out." Although talking it out may be helpful for some students, it's not for all students. Simply talking about a traumatic experience can be retraumatizing and generate negative feelings that are difficult to deal with.

Bill, a grown adult, can't talk about his sister's death from breast cancer 10 years ago without being overcome by emotion; he's still working through feelings of grief and loss. If a middle-aged adult without ACEs carries such strong remnants of trauma, the same is even more true for kids when they are asked to describe or share their trauma. They often become disconnected, angry, saddened, depressed, or sink back to how they coped with the trauma in the first place. It's important to leave the talking about trauma to the counselors and psychologists who are trained in how to work with children affected by trauma.

👥 Reflecting on Retraumatizing Students

Remember, as a school leader working to support students who are affected by trauma, your goal is to not retrigger, resurface, or hurt students again.

In this chapter, we've encouraged you to consider and reflect on whether the actions of educators at your school are hurting or helping children who have experienced ACEs. The hurting may be unintentional; sometimes, however, good intentions can set back a student's healing process. Examine your own thinking, beliefs, practices, interactions, and work to become a more trauma-sensitive educator who is supporting, uplifting, and inspiring students affected by trauma.

- Are you sensitive to the social and emotional needs of your students?
- Do you communicate in a way that demonstrates care and empathy?
- Do you encourage teachers to provide choice in learning experiences for students?
- Do your interactions reflect that you are aware that students in your school have had ACEs?
- How much do you know about the social-emotional wellness of the students in your school?
- How has this chapter challenged you as an educator?

Gather your grade-level partners, school leadership team, cabinet, or any other collaborative group and discuss your reflections on the content of this chapter.

3

Discipline
Practices

Embracing a Supportive,
Solution-Based Approach

*Remember, no matter the problem, kindness is always the right
response. When your child is having a problem, stop, listen,
then respond to the need, not the behavior. The behavior can be
addressed later, after the need has been met, because only then
is the door to effective communication truly open.*

—L. R. Knost—
*Whispers Through Time: Communication Through
the Ages and Stages of Childhood*

Many common discipline practices cause more problems than they prevent, and this is especially so for students affected by trauma. Fortunately, school leaders have the power to transform student discipline into a catalyst for positive change. In this chapter, we highlight the types of discipline practices that need to be abandoned and provide practical strategies that you can implement in your school to establish a safer, more positive, and sustainable learning environment.

Dave likes to remind both himself and the students and staff members at his school that the most salient part of discipline is connected to teaching and learning. The root of the word *discipline* comes from the Latin word for *pupil* (*discipulus*). No matter what choices and resulting actions you are facing, each student discipline situation is an opportunity for you to learn. Listen in order to understand, suspend judgment, admit your errors, reflect on other options you could have chosen, and use that new learning going forward.

When faced with an incident requiring disciplinary action, does your mind often jump to who was "right," what you need to do so this will never happen again, or how your reputation will be strengthened or tarnished if you lessen any consequences? These are not the best questions to ask. In Chapter 1, we encouraged you to replace "What's wrong with you?" with "What happened to you?"—a mindset shift that signals you're open to considering the widespread effects of trauma and supporting students who have experienced trauma. Ablon (2020) put it this way:

> Students who exhibit challenging behavior are often the students with trauma histories because being exposed to chronic stress or trauma delays brain development, causing lags in skill development which in turn result in challenging behaviors. As a direct result of their trauma, many of these students struggle with skills

like flexibility, frustration tolerance, and problem-solving. They don't lack the will to behave well; they lack the *skills* to behave well. (para. 3)

School Discipline Practices to Change

As Ablon (2020) noted, "Traditional school discipline revolves around rewarding students when they do what we want and revoking privileges when they don't" (para. 3). This does not meet the needs of students who have been affected by trauma. Far too often, educators see exerting power over students—being "tough" or "strong" on student discipline—as a way to gain compliance and cooperation. Perhaps they learned this behavior from the teachers they had in school. Other educators constantly award and take away student privileges (often pitting one student against another or against the entire class), stripping away the hope of growth and progress and stirring up blame and resentment.

Authoritarian educators try to gain compliance through fear, intimidation, or manipulation. In a school that Bill worked in, there was a teacher nicknamed "the yeller." This teacher could go from zero to 60 faster than a Tesla. It was common for this teacher to single out students and belittle them in front of their peers. Like many authoritarian teachers, the yeller had a "slippery slope" philosophy of discipline: if one kid was "allowed" to get away with something, soon every kid would be testing boundaries and trying to undercut teacher authority. It was therefore, in this teacher's mind, imperative to do whatever was necessary to demonstrate control and maintain power.

A "zero tolerance" discipline policy in the hands of an authoritarian teacher can alter a student's entire educational trajectory—by expulsion, obviously, but also by shutting the door on positive disciplinary approaches that could help that student develop valuable prosocial and self-regulatory behaviors. In the words of van der Kolk (2014),

> It is standard practice in many schools to punish children for tantrums, spacing out or aggressive outbursts—all of which are symptoms of traumatic stress. When that happens, the school, instead of offering a safe haven, becomes yet another traumatic trigger. Angry confrontations and punishment can at best temporarily halt unacceptable behaviors, but since the underlying alarm systems and stress hormones are not laid to rest, they are certain to erupt again at the next provocation. (p. 353)

A student who has been abused by a parent, emotionally scarred by a relative, sexually abused by a coach, or violently attacked by an older adult will have substantial setbacks in this type of education setting. When teachers raise their voices, shout at students, or become enraged, some students might be reminded of the time their father abused their mom, the incessant verbal fighting between their parents, or the drunken family member who became violent.

There are very few times teachers need to raise their voices in school. There is *never* a time to yell at a kid in a demeaning or derogatory manner. Raising your voice to stop a fight, to intervene for safety, or to gain the attention of a large crowd can be productive if done in a caring, loving, and professional manner.

With these "don'ts" fresh in mind, let's switch gears to focus on the do's: principles that should guide your efforts to revamp discipline practices to be kinder and less triggering to students living with trauma.

▶ Reflect, Regulate, and Rise Above

Have you ever come home from school frustrated and still upset from parents or staff members disparaging your leadership or personally attacking you in front of others? It is important to be able to rise above these kinds of encounters and move forward without allowing them to drive your decision making and affect your personal life. Consider this: have you ever been short-tempered with your own children, distant and silent from your spouse or partner, or sad and disconnected from your friends—as a result of a student's actions at school? Your time away from school is an important opportunity to "refuel" for the next day(s) ahead.

In your disciplinary interactions with students, it's essential to remain emotionally regulated (Souers & Hall, 2020); but, of course, it's difficult (if not impossible) to be emotionally regulated when you take students' behavior personally. It clouds your judgment, skews your thinking, and can trigger emotions like anger and resentment toward students. When you get emotionally charged, you lose your focus—increasing the risk that your words and actions might be traumatizing. Figure 3.1 provides a scale of levels of response to student behavior. Where do you fall on the line?

3.1 Reflection: Are You Taking It Personally?

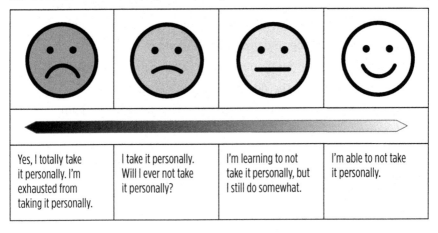

| Yes, I totally take it personally. I'm exhausted from taking it personally. | I take it personally. Will I ever not take it personally? | I'm learning to not take it personally, but I still do somewhat. | I'm able to not take it personally. |

Carol Ann Tomlinson (2020) recommends that educators "don't ever assume a student's behavior is about you," explaining that "as long as that's your frame, a student's worth is somehow an indicator of your own" (p. 32). Maintaining focus and emotional regulation enables you to see beyond the negative behavior to the student underneath the surface of poor decisions. And you may have to let it go and start afresh each time you are working with that student. If you don't start afresh, you risk letting past actions cloud your judgment and become a driving force in disciplining that student.

By letting go and not taking students' actions personally, you're able to treat each action separately and objectively support students in a way that empowers their learning and inspires hope. For students affected by trauma, this is especially important: you are providing them with a caring and loving adult who sees them for who they are—rather than what they can give, what they can't do, or how they cannot be trusted.

▶ Teach the Skills of Behavior

It can be tempting to throw the power card when frustrated with a student in a discipline conference. Many times, the underlying assumption is that the student failed to demonstrate the desired behavior because they simply did not want to. This is an easy way to get exasperated and drawn into a power struggle!

Remember Ablon (2020) distinguishing the will to behave from the skills of behavior? Instead of the adults in your school imposing *their* will on students to produce an occasional, fleeting correct behavior, they should focus on helping students to build skills so they can own and control their behavior in a new way. Ablon and Pollastri (2018) have recommended using "the research in the neurosciences to help explain what is actually getting in the way for students . . . to help educators rethink challenging behavior as a deficit of *skill,* not *will*" (p. xi). Think of student behavior in this way: it is not a matter of will but a lack of skills that's causing the acting out, misbehavior, and poor decision making.

Students who constantly are acting out in school lack the skills to overcome their negative behaviors. Their teachers need to come alongside them, teach them how to process their behaviors, and provide concrete and practical ways to behave as an alternative to continuing down their path of chronic misbehavior. Programs like Positive Behavior Interventions and Supports (PBIS) can be a powerful way to replace misbehavior with habits for success. The Center for PBIS (www.pbis.org) has many resources available online. Restorative practices is a social science that shows how important it is to spend time repairing a broken relationship before a student is simply returned to an environment that's likely to produce a similar, unwanted behavior or response. The International Institute for Restorative Practices (www.iirp.edu) has resources to help you get started. When students are explicitly taught to self-regulate, resolve conflict, work through frustration, and make amends for harmful actions, they build the skills and confidence they need to become successful and responsible adults.

▶ Suspend Judgment

Is there any basis or justification for being quick to judge students for their actions? Suspending judgment demonstrates care and concern for students' well-being. There was a student who fell asleep every day in Bill's class. It turned out that this student wasn't lazy and checking out: he was staying up late to support his family and their multiple needs. This information gave Bill a fresh perspective on this student and provided a different way to look at his sleeping in class. Being truly trauma-informed requires suspending judgment and moving toward showing care and concern. Paul Gorski (2020), founder of the Equity Literacy Institute, wrote in *Educational Leadership*,

> If a child accrues a bunch of tardies, we must withhold judgment and show concern. If a child comes to school high, we must withhold judgment and show concern. Whatever a child does, the trauma-informed response is to make sure everybody is safe, then withhold judgment and show concern. (p. 19)

Try to avoid a first reaction of punishment for poor behavior; instead, seek to understand the underlying cause and show concern for students as individuals.

▶ Look Beyond Your Own Norms

In Chapter 1, we encouraged you to think about underlying biases—your own and those that your teachers might hold. One typical assumption, unspoken and unacknowledged, is that students and their educators have the same values, experiences, and expectations when it comes to "proper" behavior. If you grew up in a home where conflict was resolved through talking it out in a calm and controlled manner, it's easy to feel anger and frustration when a student gets loud while trying to resolve a conflict or during an emotional time. This student may have grown up in a home that was loud, and being loud was how problems were resolved. Being able to see students' behavior as "different" rather than "wrong" is an important step in understanding and accepting students' diverse experiences and needs.

Using your trauma-informed lens, consider the teacher who asks students to speak up and share what's bothering them or says,

"Look at me when I'm talking to you." Some students affected by trauma shut down when confronted by adults and can become mute rather than speaking their true feelings. Their experience tells them that if they speak up, they will get beaten down. If you did not experience trauma as a kid, you may not understand how difficult it can be for these students to interact with someone representing power and authority. Be sensitive, calm, and caring, and show concern for that student.

A true trauma-informed focus on discipline demonstrates empathy for students and acknowledges students' diverse backgrounds and experiences. This approach is culturally responsive; how committed are you to learning about the cultures of your students? The students in your school are from a wide range of cultures and experiences, with different practices, social norms and cues, and values. Embrace the idea of diversity as a celebration of these differences; it's what makes each of your students unique.

▶ Praise More Often Than You Punish

How often do you and your staff praise or positively reinforce the behaviors you want to see with students? When was the last time that you recognized, honored, or celebrated students for following the rules, doing what's expected of them, or going above and beyond to help others? Using only punitive discipline consequences in an effort to correct students' behavior is "about as trauma-uninformed and trauma-insensitive as it gets" (Ablon, 2020, para. 4). Often, students who have experienced trauma also have grown accustomed to being put down, minimized, or insulted—at home and in school. As Ablon observes,

> Nowhere in the trauma-informed practice literature have I seen
> anyone advocate for the use of power and control to manipulate

a traumatized student's behavior. Using behavior charts and rewards and consequences is doing just that. It is leveraging a power differential to increase compliance. (para. 4)

Flip the script and praise kids more than punish them. Focus on finding good in all students, celebrate the good, and nurture the continuation of good behavior. Make it your goal to find the good in your students—especially those who chronically make poor decisions—and help them to flourish.

Bill's school started a "positive principal referral" system that celebrates and honors students for living out the school community's core values (i.e., demonstrating great behavior). Staff members write the referrals and the principals present students with a certificate, take their picture for social media, and contact their parents. Parents love getting these kinds of calls and the opportunity to hear how their kids are doing great things, students feel recognized and honored, and the community as a whole gets to celebrate the collective good. The students know that getting called to the office is not necessarily a bad thing—it's been a great way to make a positive connection with them. For students who have not been taught positive social skills, a program like this offers an organic way for them to see positive behaviors in action—and the way they are praised and encouraged.

Programs such as these are a powerful part of shaping a school's culture. Focusing on the positives diminishes the mistakes, mishaps, and errors that kids make. It lifts up their strengths and celebrates the good that they are doing. The key is to make sure you are not just celebrating and honoring the kids who are achieving at the highest academic levels or avoiding discipline referrals. Sure, these students deserve recognition, but fragile and struggling learners also deserve and need to be celebrated. In implementing this type of positive-behavior program, use your student information system to ensure that you are awarding accolades evenly, in a way that reflects your school's demographics. (For example, at first, the positive principal referral program was recognizing way more female students than male students—10:1!) Sharing such data (e.g., race, ethnicity, socioeconomic status) with staff helps ensure your program will be equitable.

▶ Distinguish Between Behaving and Learning

Educators can fall into the trap of believing that the most powerful tool they have to influence a student's behavior is through grading, and by grading behavior, they are teaching students responsibility. So they deduct points for that late paper, fail an entire project group because of one student's misbehavior, or give a student a zero for never handing in work. This approach is easy, it's black-and-white, cut-and-dried, a convenient tool for gaining control in the classroom. Putting aside for a moment the effect this might have on behavior, what effect does this have on the real objective, which is promoting student learning? Do any of these practices—deducting points for misbehavior, giving a zero for missing work, downgrading a paper for not being neat, deducting points for a missing name or class period—encourage student learning? Does it align with the purpose of assessment, which is to gauge students' attainment of a skill, concept, or standard in order to promote their attainment of that learning?

Blurring the lines of reporting academic success and reporting behavior deprives students, their parents, their teachers, and their school leaders an accurate picture of their understanding and mastery. A student's behavior is not a reflection of intellectual capacity.

For students who experience trauma, incorporating behavior into grading creates an even more inaccurate representation of who they are intellectually. As we have noted, often conditions outside the school day prevent a student from doing what's highly valued in some gradebooks (e.g., homework, extra-credit items, last-minute assignments), which results in a grade that does not necessarily reflect whether a student grasps the content. The result? Students start to believe that their academic ability is poor and their understanding weak. This, in turn, may produce a downward spiral where falling confidence leads to diminished effort and eventually prevents the ability to attain desired learning outcomes. Students may start to demonstrate avoidance behaviors, sometimes simply out of embarrassment. They want to do the very things that their out-of-school life prevents them from accomplishing.

▶ Give Every Student a Clean Slate

In our advice to not take students' behavior personally and "let it go," we encouraged you to consider each new disciplinary encounter with students a fresh start.

When Bill was a teacher, a colleague mentioned that the kids in Bill's first period class had been a significant discipline challenge for him the year before. "That might have been the worst class I ever had," the colleague confided. "Those kids made my life a living nightmare." When teachers give a lot of weight to students' "reputations," it's easy to conclude that nothing can be done, that "that's who these kids are." In Figure 3.2, we list some comments that indicate bias against students that's rooted in past behavior and might encourage other teachers to write off individual (or groups of) students without ever getting to know them. How often do you hear these sorts of comments in your school?

3.2 Reflection on Behavior Bias: Staff Comments to Students

Instructions: Reflect on the frequency of each statement's occurrence at your school.			
Statement	I've heard this a lot	I've heard this once or twice	Our staff would never say this
This is the worst ever ___th grade class to come through this school.			
Our school was so much better before that new housing development went in.			
That kid is the worst I have ever had in all my years of teaching.			
That new kid from _____ is someone we need to watch out for.			
Every student on that bus is a behavior problem in our school.			
That kid, _____, is never going to change.			
I taught that kid's brother; the family is trouble.			
Don't let other kids hang out with _____; she's just going to pull them down.			
Notes			

This type of talk has no place in a school. When teachers choose to listen to and embrace the negativity that is handed down year to year, they help to perpetuate negative behaviors and actions. Students whose lives are affected by trauma are not given an opportunity for a fresh start or new beginning; they continue to be held back by the expectations of educators rather than being set free to begin anew. Commit to looking at each student, every year, as a new slate ready for your teaching team to invest in and inspire every day.

A clean slate—a new beginning, a fresh start—is an essential element of the student discipline process in the trauma-informed school. Students need to feel valued. *Conditional value* focuses on a condition or something that students can do—not based on the individual person. Just the opposite should be true: educators should unconditionally value students. *Unconditional value* is based on the person regardless of actions, conditions, or behaviors. This mindshift supports and acknowledges students for who they are and not what they can do. Achieving the status of teacher's pet, coach's favorite point guard, or band instructor's prized player is often based on how well a student is complying with what the adult wants or meeting the adult's expectations. Teachers also fall prey to promoting conditional value for what students might do in the future—a coach places high value on a student who might one day play in the NFL, a science teacher sees a future doctor in the classroom, the principal touts how many of the graduating class applied to Ivy League schools. These students are more valued than someone who is failing a course, does not participate in extracurricular activities, or who gets a job right out of high school. We encourage you to heed Carol Ann Tomlinson's (2020) admonition: "No kid's worth is tied up in grammar lessons, algebraic formulas, or any other content knowledge. Kids need to know that" (p. 32).

▶ Speak Encouragement into the Lives of Students

Far too often, students—especially students who have experienced trauma—have had negativity, discouragement, and reminders of failures spoken, whispered, and shouted to them. These words can have a tremendous impact, everything from intensifying students' learning struggles to leading them to act out against classroom norms. This is why it's so important for all educators to speak words of encouragement into the lives of students. Encouragement, reassurance, and honest compliments based on good work and promising habits can release the negative thoughts and ideas that imprison so many students and trick them into believing they are worthless, doomed to failure, or a disappointment.

Try to use some of these phrases to uplift and inspire your students: *I believe in you, you got this, you are enough, I love your work ethic, I'm here to support you, you are more than your latest test score,* and *you are amazing.* Model this way of speaking for staff, and be clear that you expect all staff to follow your example.

If you should learn that a staff member is using sarcasm with students, ridiculing them, or making any student feel "less than" through words and deeds, intervene immediately to stop this type of behavior. Yes, even if it's from teachers who have many years in the district, are respected by their peers, or are liked by students. Trauma-informed leadership leaves no room for denigration.

▶ Put Relationships First

In an interview in *Educational Leadership,* Nadine Burke-Harris described the importance of providing "stable nurturing relationships and environments that we know are healing. That involves moving away from punitive consequences for certain behaviors and more toward interventions that are healing" (Thiers, 2020, p. 12).

The most effective discipline takes place within a positive, nurturing, and caring relationship, one that values the power of conversation. The conversation must focus on listening, building a connection, and inspiring real and positive change. Between the four of us, we have been in thousands of discipline conferences with students. Productive discipline student conferences are based on trust, a caring relationship, and a commitment to unlocking the best in kids. Author Eric Jensen (2016) sums it up like this: "Seek first to understand, leave the judging aside. To keep coming to school, students need a caring adult, not a judge and an executioner" (p. 48).

In our experience, students who have been affected by trauma value educators who are willing to focus on relationships first. These educators see a discipline incident as an episode rather than an indication of character. They are committed to building up the person and ensuring that the student feels cared for, loved, and supported. Doing this allows students to open up, share, and learn. Students who have been affected by trauma feel safe and are able to express themselves in a way that promotes healthy relationship skills far into the future.

The trust that is established between a student and educator can help to break down some of the barriers that trauma causes. When students know that a teacher, counselor, or principal really cares about them as a person, they see that they are valued in a way that may be new to them. As Jessica Minahan (2020) has noted, "The impact of trauma can be lifelong, so what students learn during this school year ultimately won't be as important as whether they feel safe" (para. 3).

"Trauma-invested practice is . . . the art of bringing the human element back into education" (Souers & Hall, 2020, p. 39). This human element relies on a nurturing, caring, and loving relationship between students and educators. What ways can you strengthen relationships within the student discipline models of your school? Figure 3.3 provides some guidance for approaching common student discipline activities using a trauma-informed lens.

Educators cannot prevent students from experiencing trauma, but they can be intentional in designing discipline systems to

3.3 Discipline Practices Through a Relationships Lens

Practice	Questions to Consider
Student discipline conferences	• Do these conferences provide a time for conversation, or are they one-way directives to the student? • Do these conferences build a connection with students or push them farther away? • Do these conferences help students understand their actions or simply deliver punishment? • Do these conferences help students feel supported or punished for their actions?
Phone calls to family members	• Are these opportunities to build relationships with families, or do they solely provide notification of a discipline infraction? • Are these calls a chance to provide support to the family, or do they highlight how the student's caregivers have failed? • Are these calls a time to show care and support for the family and student or a way to reinforce school rules? • Are these calls an opportunity to provide additional school and community resources or a quick call to only state the facts?
Teachers' approach to discipline	• Do teachers show care and concern for students, or are they focused on reinforcing their rules? • Do teachers help students understand how to make better decisions or punish them for making poor decisions? • Do teachers provide hope for a fresh start or remind students of their past failures? • Do teachers understand how trauma affects students, or do they ignore trauma and see it as an excuse for poor decisions?
Student referral system	• Do discipline referrals include emotionally charged words, opinions, or absolutes written by teachers, or are they factually based? • Do discipline referrals only focus on punishment and not intervention? • Do discipline referrals focus on the infraction and not the person? • Do discipline referrals consider the trauma experienced by students?

better support, protect, and care for students who have experienced trauma. School administrators who are committed to being trauma-informed are constantly reflecting, growing, and identifying ways to empower students.

Many outdated and hurtful practices that are pervasive in schools can trigger trauma in students and diminish their performance. We challenge you to reflect on your school's student discipline practices and identify ways to transition to a trauma-informed approach that supports students and empowers them to thrive in their school, home, community, and world.

👥 Reflecting on Discipline Practices

In this chapter, we've encouraged you to consider how well your discipline practices align with a trauma-informed approach—one that respects students, provides hope and encouragement, is restorative in nature, and works to help them get back on track to learning and progress. We recognize that making this shift will have its challenges; there may be adults in your building who will cling to traditional ways. It's important, too, to assess your own thinking, where your strengths lie, where you need to improve, and how you want to move forward.

- Are you able to not take student behavior personally?
- Do you work to empower students by teaching them replacement behaviors and providing the supports they need?
- Are you open to understanding the diverse experiences and perspectives of students who are different from you?
- Do you offer praise and recognize good behavior?
- Do your teachers avoid factoring behavior into their grading practices?

Gather your school leadership team, cabinet, or any other collaborative group and discuss your reflections on the content of this chapter.

Learning Spaces

Redesigning the Environment for Greater Safety and Support

Today's education system faces irrelevance unless we bridge
the gap between how students live and how students learn.

—Partnership for 21st Century Skills—

Before becoming a school counselor, Andrea was an elementary school teacher. She found that classroom design was important in welcoming kids and giving them a sense of ownership of their learning space. She wanted them to love coming to school!

Around the building, Andrea's classroom was known as "Studio 214." It had desks, but it also had lots of optional seating around the room, including theater seats. There were stools, crate chairs, and bouncy balls that were all used for flexible seating. Andrea got rid of her huge teacher workstation and purchased a standing desk that students used during class time. Students were able to complete tasks with partners and chose where they sat. This theme of flexibility permeated everything students did in the classroom. Andrea used music to signal cleanup and transitions, to help students learn material or take brain breaks, and to calm and take moments to be mindful. All of these things cost little money but had a huge effect on classroom culture and how kids felt about being in the room together.

Some classrooms in Andrea's school have now gotten rid of *all* student desks and use alternate seating and tables to create a more inviting atmosphere. The school library also has spaces intended to help students feel calm and safe: a reading area with an open, specially lit tent, where kids can sit in a comfy chair to read, and a "create space," where kids create something. The create-space station includes blank hardcover books, stationery, card kits, origami, art supplies, and bracelet-making materials. The library office has a new calming corner for staff and students, with rocking chairs and a couch, along with fidget toys and coloring books.

When Andrea set out to create a comfortable, welcoming space in her school counselor's office, she wanted it to feel as homey as possible. She purchased furniture that she would use in her home and even brought pieces from her home to help furnish it. When her younger students visit, some of them actually believe she lives there and refers to it as her house.

So that's Andrea's space, Andrea's school. What about yours?

When was the last time you took a walk through your school and saw it through the eyes of your students? Is the school cluttered, too busy? Are the halls or classrooms crowded or chaotic? Little things can make a big difference when it comes to streamlining an area and making it feel calm. Can supplies be put away out of sight? Is the posted artwork and information useful and pleasing, or is it too much? Visual stimulation can be a trigger for some students who have experienced trauma. When you walk through your campus, what do you smell? Is the building inviting, or does it send a different message? What textures are used throughout? Are there rugs and areas in your building that feel like home, or do most of the spaces seem cold?

Also consider what you hear. Are teachers using calm voices to address students? Is there music playing? These are important aspects to think about when redesigning spaces on your campus— key to making your school inviting and calming for students. Figure 4.1 is a checklist to help guide your observations and pinpoint necessary improvements.

Why Redesign Learning Spaces?

Kids who face trauma benefit greatly from a school where leaders have closely examined how to use their space, seating, and class setup to support learning. It's time for leaders to rethink how every inch of space in a school is used and consider how the physical space can be reset to foster relationship building, empower flexibility, and create spaces that are more private and reflective for students. How can learning spaces best support the needs of students? How can the school carve out areas for quiet reflection and support? How can classrooms, cafeterias, hallways, and open spaces be reconfigured to foster comfort and well-being? Consider swapping out the traditional desks. What other kinds of furniture might eliminate barriers, nurture engagement, and foster relaxation? Look for ways to integrate rocking chairs, beanbag chairs, stand-up desks, and large tables for group collaboration.

4.1 Reflection: Building Walk-Through

Focus Points	No	Mostly	Yes
Instructions: Reflect on the accuracy of the statements. In the Notes column, be precise about areas that need to be improved. Where are they? In what ways do spaces need to be improved? How could you do this?			
The school is clean, organized, and clutter-free.			
The school appears to be safe and orderly.			
The hallways are bright, colorful, and welcoming.			
The school has a variety of seating and furniture options.			
The sounds in the school are calming.			
The school has a home-like feel to it.			
There is soft and soothing music playing.			
Pictures in the school reflect the demographics of the school.			
It is easily identifiable how students can seek help and support (e.g., on bulletin boards, walls).			
It sounds like people are having fun (e.g., laughing, giggling).			
Notes			

Redesign is more than just swapping out the furniture. It's about intentionally considering the needs of students. Create a reflection or support space (or room) where students can go when they are feeling anxious. Provide an alternative to the large cafeteria for lunchtime. Identify safe areas in the school where kids can go to find support, take time to meditate or reflect, and refocus. Students struggling with trauma often need time to de-escalate, decompress, and reengage after something during the typical school day inadvertently activates a fight-or-flight response.

Redesign can be powerful when a teacher changes an individual classroom, but it gains even more effectiveness when the entire school staff engages in the process of examining, and redesigning, the spaces in every classroom and large-group areas. For a true trauma-informed redesign to happen, leaders need to consider key areas: leveraging human and financial resources, meeting students' mental health needs, and repurposing the school's physical space.

Best Practices in Redesign

Identifying partners with experience in design can be a very effective way to create change. Schools in Pennsylvania are fortunate to have a connection with a regional resource called an "intermediate unit." The one in Bill and Dave's school district sponsors sessions with a commercial designer that specializes in flexible meeting spaces and adaptable learning spaces. Such a firm is essential for a major project, but don't overlook the power of the designers already in your school. Meet with your art teachers, engineering staff, and facilities department, and get their input. While you are gathering suggestions for your spaces, don't forget to include student voices. Students are likely to add a perspective that others will not consider, and ultimately the success of your design will play out in your students' experiences.

All of your design conversations should focus on what you are trying to build, together. This is more than just the walls, ceilings, and floor. What kinds of academic, social-emotional, and wellness outcomes do you have in mind? How will these spaces provide support for all students? Universal design for learning (UDL) can play a role here, especially when considered in the light of the historical barriers and systemic racism that add to the anxiety and trauma experienced by Black and Brown students. Author Andratesha Fritzgerald (2020) has stressed that schools must become safe relationally and emotionally for Black students before they can become safe academically. Her question for educators is "Do you stereotype different groups of students based on what you think they are like, or what you think they will like?" (p. 43). Keeping your students in the conversation, soliciting their feedback, and inviting a diversity of opinions will help ensure that your resulting actions are effective.

Some of the spaces that need to be designed (or redesigned) are not physical spaces at all. The recent need for virtual learning spaces has shown that support for students does not need to end when they leave the school building. How do you offer opportunities in your learning management system, communication software, and other technology-based resources to allow students to share their questions, concerns, struggles, and fears with adults in your school? Can students easily ask their teachers for help without other students knowing? Does every student know they can express concern for their own well-being (or a friend's) using a tip line, suicide prevention hotline, or similar intervention? The digital divide, which was exposed during the COVID-19 pandemic, has widened the gap between learners, putting those who were already disadvantaged at increased risk of falling behind their peers. Lack of technology or internet at home has, in some ways, deepened students' disconnection with the school community.

Online spaces and resources are not limited to student support. Does your human resources department extend support to professional and nonprofessional staff, by providing services such as resources for health care, mental health counseling, life coaching, and wellness? Can your teachers receive a discount at a local health club or fitness facility? If these opportunities don't exist, encourage

your district to pursue them. Adults who are physically and emotionally healthy have more to offer students. When adults are not
well, the effects ripple through the entire system. As the saying goes,
"Hurt people hurt people. "

▶ Leverage Human Resources to Support Students

The strongest, most effective resource you have in your school is
your staff. People make the difference. Research such as that conducted by Hattie and Yates (2014) has demonstrated that, of factors
relating to student achievement, teacher efficacy has the greatest
impact. And teachers make a difference in areas outside academic
achievement; that same student–teacher relationship can be foundational when helping students address anxiety, depression, negative self-talk, and other barriers to learning. With the help of other
caring adults and peers, the time spent in school can be hours of
support and healing to address a lifetime of traumatic experiences
and their long-lasting effects. Teachers affect students' lives for over
14,000 hours in the journey from kindergarten to graduation—and
this doesn't even consider the thousands of hours many students
spend in after-school programs and activities.

Adults make a difference, and scheduling those adults so your
strongest teachers, aides, and counselors have the most time with
your most fragile learners is an important strategy. Don't automatically assign your "best teacher" to the "best learners." Doing this
may please and support some adults in the building, but it hurts the
kids. Put your most highly relational adults with your most fragile students—and make sure that students who have experienced
trauma are with these teachers and staffers as well. When you do
this, you cultivate a culture that truly puts the needs of kids first.

▶ Provide Spaces with Mental Health Needs in Mind

Increasing flexible seating options and designing collaborative spaces are legitimate areas on which to focus, but you also need to think about redesigning your school to include other kinds of space. What could areas designed specifically to allow kids to de-escalate look like? Perhaps this would be, in an elementary school, a playroom that encourages some physical movement (think: a Wii or bean-bag toss game). Even if you don't have a dedicated playroom, you might set up a bean-bag toss near the main office outside the principal's door so students who need to unwind can use it, or outside on the sidewalk or playground. The benefits of play are well documented (Getz, 2011; Gil, 2010). Getz has pointed out that "children can work on issues that are distressing to them, can play out issues of what the future will be, and can talk about trauma. If it's too hard to put into words, they can work on it with play" (p. 20). Whether this space is a dedicated room or a ping-pong table in your main lobby, consider ways to expand access to play—especially for our older students who no longer have recess in their daily schedule.

A primary school counselor in Virginia shared with us how she focuses on the mental health needs of her students:

> Last year we made calm-down kits and paired them with a Big Joe bean-bag chair to have in every room in the building (classrooms, library, office, etc.) so that students know there is a safe space no matter where they are. The kit contains a variety of sensory materials, SEL books, and a sand timer to help them self-regulate. As the counselor, I've created individual kits for kiddos to keep near their desks and even sent some kits home with information for the guardian about how to use and why.

A Mindfulness Room

A "mindfulness room" is another space to consider. This space could be equipped with diffusers to calm the lighting, a Bluetooth speaker with calming music or environmental sounds, an aquarium (or video loop of an aquarium), and some comfortable seating. This space allows students to find a way to escape any tension and fear building up because of something happening in the school. Posters on the wall might remind students of breathing exercises or mantras (e.g., "This too shall pass," "My fear does not define me").

What if you had a room in your school where a student who is feeling troubled could visit and spend time with a therapy dog? (Maybe a therapy guinea pig would be easier to implement, but you get the idea.) Animal-assisted therapy has many benefits including improvement in cardiac function, neuroendocrine (stress hormone) activation, and psychological changes in mood (Gawlinski & Steers, 2005). The UCLA School of Health (2020) concludes that "the simple act of petting animals releases an automatic relaxation response." This response includes the positive benefits of the release of serotonin, prolactin, and oxytocin—all hormones that can play a part in elevating mood. Therapy dogs can also help people lower anxiety, relax, be comforted, and feel less lonely. These interactions also increase mental stimulation, including providing an escape or happy distraction, or acting as catalysts in the therapy process to help break the ice, reducing the initial resistance that might accompany therapy.

Although the addition of a full-time therapy dog or similar animal may be prohibitive to implement, the addition of a robotic animal might produce similar benefits. (University of Portsmouth, 2020). A robotic companion may be much more attainable for your school, and it is a way for you to ensure your students (and staff) benefit from the outcomes of animal-assisted therapy.

A Music Room

A music room may also have a space in your school. We're not referring to the choral, band, or orchestra room. Consider a space in your school where simple percussion instruments and other tools to unwind and create are available for students. We're sure you've experienced how songs can energize, inspire, and soothe. Music has the power to reach a deep level and can be very effective in calming anxiety. A space that includes an iPad with headphones or a speaker system may be all that's needed to give students a creative environment that provides the momentary relief they need before reengaging with their teachers and peers after a trauma-induced setback. Consider loading an app like GarageBand that offers both musicians and nonmusicians access to the mood-altering magic of creating music as well as listening to it, and reinforces the message that your school is a diverse, trauma-sensitive, responsive place for all learners. Bill's high school doesn't have a dedicated music therapy space, but there is a piano in the main lobby. Students are free to sit and play, and the rest of the school benefits from that music ringing in the air.

A LEGO Wall

Bill's high school also has a LEGO wall in the library for students to tinker, explore, and create. Students will often walk through the library, pick up some LEGOs, and add to the creation already there. This is a simple, fun, and inexpensive (all the LEGO bricks at Dave's school were donated by families looking to get rid of them) way to establish some downtime for kids. A LEGO wall provides an outlet, escape, or retreat from daily challenges. Everyone in the school can contribute to the wall, adults and kids alike, and the LEGO wall is also a tool to bring people together in a playful and inviting way.

Outside Spaces

When redesigning spaces, don't forget to think outside the buildings as well. At Andrea's elementary school, they have redesigned a courtyard area in recent years to include seating where students can work on assignments or just enjoy eating outside together during lunch or snack. They also created an outdoor eating area with large tables and colorful umbrellas that classes reserve each day so students can get fresh air and just have a different atmosphere in which to eat and talk to each other. There are plans to create an outdoor garden area as well, made possible by a grant the school received from a local nonprofit partnership. Being outside and gardening are both great ways students and adults can practice self-care and be a great addition to school campuses at minimal cost.

Outside areas of learning can be redesigned or transformed by students, too. Empower them to design the gardens, plant the trees, or help build the outdoor eating area. These types of places and activities provide students who have experienced trauma an outlet for their struggles and a place to gain mindfulness while at school.

Changes in Lighting

Many schools have bright, fluorescent lighting, which is not very inviting, especially when trying to create a warm atmosphere in which students feel comfortable and calm. Lighting can be adjusted by dimming the lights, adding some lamps around the classroom, or covering fluorescent lights with film covers. Andrea, who purchased light covers for her office's harsh ceiling lights, can testify to the huge difference it makes. Similarly, when Bill and Dave worked at the same middle school, the autism support teacher there used light blue filters over the lights to help soften the lights and create a calmer vibe.

In what ways could you switch up the lighting in your school to be softer, warmer, and more soothing to the eyes and minds of students? Perhaps buy a bunch of string lights after the holidays to hang in classes, purchase some calming lamps, or use nightlights to softly brighten a corner of a room.

▶ Embrace Design That Reflects Your School Demographics

Jostens Renaissance Education's "The Pulse" survey (www.jostens renaissance.com) helps school administrators assess a number of components relating to school culture. After reading his students' responses to the question "Do images hanging in your hallways/ classrooms reflect your school's demographics?" Bill did a walkthrough of the school. He realized that the vast majority of pictures and photographs in the building were of white students.

Everything in the halls is now more reflective of its occupants. The school is filled with pictures that truly reflect the student body (and the world). It is important that kids are able to see themselves on the walls of your school. We know of one school that enlarges pictures of their students and pairs these with famous quotes—an excellent way to inspire students and to encourage them to greatness.

▶ Learn from Positive Examples

Industry and business have been experimenting with space redesign for years, and this experience is a great resource for your creation of seating, design, and collaborative spaces that support student learning. Figure 4.2 lists ideas from various companies that can transform a redesign. Think of how these might be applied to strengthen the learning experiences for students affected by trauma and help them to be calm, collaborative, and focused on learning. The examples we share all entice people to stay longer in the space and to return. Shouldn't your school do the same?

4.2 Redesign Ideas from the Corporate World

The Business	The Idea	Why It Works	In Your School
Cracker Barrel	Rocking chairs outside all the restaurants	Rocking chairs provide the feeling of relaxing on the front porch, hanging out with friends, and letting the worries of the world rock away.	Invest in rocking chairs for your lobby, hallways, and other areas of the school.
Starbucks	High-top tables where customers can either stand or sit to chat, work, or drink their beverage	These tables promote conversation and collaboration.	Consider installing stand-up tables in your main lobby and some of the hallways. These tables have the potential to become hubs of collaboration and an opportunity for students to simply get some work done.
	"Bringing the outdoors indoors": blending plants, fireplaces, and glass	This is a naturally calming atmosphere.	Model this by incorporating plants, water fountains, and other natural things that give students a sense of calm.
McDonald's	Playground or Funland	Provides important opportunities for play	Incorporate fun and creativity throughout the school, not just on the playground. Perhaps an indoor slide? In your main lobby, a ping-pong table, bean-bag toss, or piano?
Costco	Food samples	Encourages customers to visit all areas	Provide treats during the day, healthy snacks during learning, or free water bottles to help keep students hydrated.

▶ Proactively Repurpose Space

At the middle school where Bill and Dave worked, repurposing the physical space related directly to some new professional staff learning on trauma and resilience in the student body. Kenneth Ginsburg from the Children's Hospital of Philadelphia (CHOP) delivered a powerful keynote address that spurred us to investigate ways to help students de-escalate after an incident (Ginsburg, 2015). They realized these same measures could be used proactively to help students in distress from acting out in ways they might later regret. After learning from Dr. Ginsburg, Bill and Dave designed a quiet and reflective area where students could go to calm down, de-escalate, or just refocus and regroup. Located next to our school counseling office, the area was staffed with a trained professional ready to provide support as needed.

A Space for Quiet Reflection

Some of your students with a recognized exceptionality (i.e., those with an individualized education plan or 504 plan) may already have support from and access to staff members or resource rooms. However, adverse childhood experiences are not limited to exceptional students; they extend broadly among students and staff.

Bill and Dave realized it was especially important to create more de-escalation spaces so anyone who needed that support would have it. An unused area near the school counselors' offices was separated from a nearby student hallway and adjacent to the main office. The purchase of two comfortable chairs, one opaque curtain, and a cheap curtain rod allowed us to transform this "unused area" into a space for a student or staff member to find a quiet, appropriately private area for reflection and retreat.

A bonus feature of this new space was the ease of access to skilled school counselors and psychologists. Many of the students who used our reflection area did indeed seek some support from these professionals. Many others benefitted from the "informal counseling" provided by building secretaries, student aides, or building administrators who were genuinely concerned and attuned to a student's proactive choice to pause and reflect. The adults in our school became more aware of how pervasive past traumatic experiences were for the students and their colleagues, and acted to help mitigate their effects in school. The small step of creating a quiet space marked the beginning of a renewed focus to care more deeply, and purposefully, for our students' social and emotional well-being.

A Space for Work and Conversation

The success of the quiet reflection space led us to consider other areas in the school that could become unique and flexible spaces. The addition of some high-top tables and chairs in the main concourse hallway allowed students to get away from a noisy, bustling cafeteria; teachers could send students outside their door to read, retest, or recollect themselves while still engaging in the learning; colleagues could find a quiet space to discuss their lessons (or their lives). By strategically placing a table and chairs adjacent to the office area, the building principal was able to move conversations outside the office walls and relax the often-held belief that you only entered the principal's office if you were in trouble.

Classroom teachers, seeing the change in the shared spaces throughout the building, began to consider ways they could incorporate similar flexibility in their own learning environments. The math department, wanting to encourage collaboration among their students, replaced traditional desks with boomerang desks that could be regrouped as singles, duos, or quads. Students who had feared math class began to respond and participate with their peers in a way that they may not have done in a whole-group setting. Language arts teachers carved out spaces to encourage reading: comfortable chairs, floor mats, benches, small dividers, and other pieces of furniture began to show up in classrooms. The science teachers realized the power of rearranging their heavy lab tables in ways that allowed students to be face-to-face instead of everyone facing the front of the room. These are simple but powerful changes that can promote healing and build healthy relationships among students.

One of the least expensive, and most immediate, changes that a school leader can make to redesign learning spaces is to encourage teachers to move the desks in their classrooms from rows to clusters. This does not require purchasing any new desks. Every subject area can benefit from creating a stronger, relational learning community. Teachers are often content to herd students quietly from the hallway into isolated rows where the intention is to ignore others, focus on what the teacher says, speak only when spoken to, and exit quietly when class is dismissed. This kind of isolation-by-design does not help a student with a history of traumatic experiences learn to interact in a healthy way. Valuing quiet compliance continues to isolate students who need to experience healthy interactions and expand their behavioral skills. Your goal is to try to ensure that all your students can be successful as they enter college, trade school, military service, or the workplace after high school.

A Space for Peer Mentoring

An unexpected benefit of these changes was realized when the positive, empathetic, and leadership-minded students at Bill and Dave's school began to act as peer mentors. Whether or not your school has an official peer mentoring or peer tutoring program, by creating environments where kids can connect with one another you will build opportunities for students to help one another. This is a reminder that the goal is not to simply rearrange the furniture, but to *redesign the support opportunities* to help students (and staff members) address the hurt they carry with them each day as they enter the building. You are redesigning spaces to build stronger relationships. When students feel connected, safe, and supported, they are in a space where they can learn and grow. This is the space where trauma's grip begins to loosen and possibilities abound.

A Space for Creativity

Redesigning school spaces can also spur innovation and creativity in learning. Allowing students to use lobbies, hallways, cafeteria spaces, courtyards, and other open areas increases opportunities for collaboration and the kind of environment where students can build healthy relationships with other students. Trusting students to work in collaborative open spaces nurtures a cooperative environment.

We are not suggesting that you simply release students anywhere in the building without supervision. It is essential to set clear expectations (see Chapter 8), have adult supervision, and establish norms in the building that promote collaboration and respect. More and more, we are seeing school leaders who are using open spaces to create collaborative "think tanks" where students can write (with washable markers) on glass windows; film videos; and otherwise come together to plan, think, converse, and deliberate over complex issues and learning.

Although it is fairly common to see elementary students working collaboratively at tables, stations, or on the floor, this flexibility seems to disappear at the secondary level. Rows become the norm and collaboration is often stifled by rigid rules and fear of misbehavior. School leaders have the opportunity to create and redesign spaces with learning, collaboration, and relationships in mind.

Simply encouraging physical movement instead of demanding stillness can help students who are feeling trapped. Why are students always seated? In the workplace, employees are frequently up and moving around, collaborating around counters, even finalizing major deals while in the open spaces of a lobby or coffee area. Spaces where students can sit on exercise-ball chairs, or desks that allow students to pedal while they sit or to rest their feet on a bar that sways back and forth, can make a positive difference. One of the social studies teachers in Dave and Bill's school placed a treadmill in her room so students could take turns walking while in class together. However old or modern your space is, it's possible to revamp how you employ it to better support student learning.

▶ Budget for Your Values

Finding adequate funding is a challenge for just about every school leader we know. Regardless of the funds available to you, it is always worthwhile to review your budget with the overriding question "What do we value?" as the guiding force. Guest speakers, for example, can bring stories of hope arising from traumatic experiences (see Chapter 8). You can seek partnerships with counseling services (see Chapter 5) to support your students and staff—there is more work than your guidance staff can possibly address. In addition to redistributing the existing funds in your annual budget, consider ways to increase revenue. If you are able to carve out some of the new spaces we suggest in this chapter, you might also find some local businesses willing to be sponsors—or perhaps school-appropriate advertisers could be added to your school or district web presence with the express intent to use that revenue in support of mental health services to address trauma.

What kinds of ongoing professional learning are you providing to staff members? Trauma, resiliency, wellness, mindfulness, and other mental health training is not simply directly related to this conversation. Building these important skills and competencies in your professional staff will also result in improved learning environments and increased achievement for your students.

Bill and Dave had the opportunity to use funds from their middle school's parent–teacher organization to provide some wellness options for staff during an in-service day. Teachers and nonprofessional staff had the chance to sign up for a variety of experiences that ranged from retirement and financial planning tips to chair massages, yoga sessions, walking for wellness, nutrition counseling, meditation and breathing strategies, and other options. This staff training went beyond the routine sessions that address instructional practices, curriculum implementation, or assessment. Based on the feedback we received after that day, and the stories that continue to resound years later, it was one of the most memorable and well-received professional learning sessions our staff ever experienced. We have been able to continue a focus on trauma-responsive schools with the help of guest speakers like Dr. Ginsburg from CHOP; staff from HopeWorks from Camden, New Jersey; and other speakers who could address the mental health issues of students and staff.

▶ Incorporate Explicitly Trauma-Informed Spaces

Dave's daughter, Laura, teaches 3rd grade at a Title I elementary school in Maryland. Many of the students have been part of the foster care system, and almost all of them have had one or more adverse childhood experiences. Three out of four students enrolled qualify for free or reduced-price lunch. Laura has been using a proactive approach with both her classroom's physical layout options and the creative materials her students can choose to use when they begin to feel their emotions interfering with their learning and their decision making.

A Sensory Room and Walk

Consider developing a "sensory room." The room at Laura's school has a blend of movement activities and sensory experiences all designed to help students take (or take back) control of their social-emotional well-being. Even if you don't have a complete room available to dedicate, you can still create a sensory space in your classroom, hallway, or other area.

A "sensory walk" in one of the hallways includes different types of movement options and other activities. First, students progress through a hopscotch grid, painted to resemble the leaves along a sunflower stalk. After completing this portion, they tiptoe through the next section, which leads them to a wall where some hand-shaped stickers give them a place to do wall push-ups. Next, they use their fingers to trace a spiral on the wall. At the end of the spiral, they're prompted to a brief crab walk. The last section gives them the choice to skip, jump, or hop the entire alphabet (displayed on the floor) and then high-five handprints on the walk to celebrate successful navigation of the walk.

Other sensory materials and physical options you might make available to students include modeling clay, a small trampoline and soft mats, pillows or cushions in a calm corner, and a "wall of textures" featuring fishbowl stones, beads on a rod over a doorway, felt, and furry fabric.

Space for Cool-Down and Choice

Teachers also can create classroom-specific spaces and intervention ideas. Dave's daughter has a "cool-down corner" where students can access a blend of active options, creativity pursuits, sensory experiences, and social-emotional learning (SEL) tools to work on their emotional regulation. This has been an effective strategy with her students who are learning to identify their emotional regulatory limits. It is also a "safe space" for students who are more withdrawn, those who don't present many physical cues, or those who are just harder to reach. Like everything else in teaching, it is important to set clear expectations for the cool-down corner, as well as modeling and practicing its intended use. It's intended to be used for short breaks.

Laura's cool-down corner offers choice in a few different categories: active movement, creativity, sensory or fidget tools, and SEL support. These allow students choice in calming strategies while keeping them mindful and responsive to their bodies. More active options might include a choice board of exercises students select to do, or a wall similar to the sensory walk where students can do wall push-ups. A variety of fidget toys and sensory tools—squishies, plush toys, marble mazes, fidget spinners, a sand tray—support students' sensory needs.

The most effective cool-down corners include SEL tools: posters depicting breathing strategies, emotion identifiers, and zones of regulation used in the school. Social storybooks, for example, often include a checklist that guides students through the process. One of our favorite options that Dave's daughter offers to students is related to their positive self-talk. She mounted a plastic mirror on the wall and surrounded the border with affirmation statements and positive self-talk strategies. She uses a dry-erase marker to include some on the mirror's surface. Students are able to have a conversation with themselves while seeing their reflection at the same time.

One last resource included in the cool-down corner (and certainly one that shouldn't be overlooked) is an "apology form." This is a reminder that time away from the class in the cool-down corner frequently begins with an outburst or other inappropriate behavior. In a caring environment, it's essential to consider how this student can be reconciled and returned to the learning community. Just rejoining the group is not nearly as effective as returning with an authentic recognition of what went wrong and an apology for those it affected.

Here are some tips from Dave's daughter for designing spaces such as cool-down corners in your school:

- Have a timer ready to start when a student needs the cool-down corner. A sand timer is a quick item to keep on hand, but a digital timer offers far more flexibility and provides an audible signal to cue you and your student when time runs out and a check-in is needed.
- Pre-teach how to use the space and what it's for (not recess), and give every student a turn to test it out. Stress that this is a tool space, not an "escape from learning" space.
- Incorporate a portable option for students who may need to use it in other spaces or to move away from peers.
- Model using the space, with your students. Have them help you choose a quiet activity from the options. Show them how using the option helps you regulate your emotions. After, have a large-group discussion about how important it is to check in with ourselves (even as adults).

👥 Reflecting on Redesign

Take a moment to consider the following questions:

- What specific space(s) in your school could be repurposed to provide a dedicated area for active movement, creative pursuits, sensory tools, and SEL supports?
- How could you redesign the faculty area to provide SEL supports and experiences for teachers and staff at your school?
- Where would you place a LEGO wall using the blocks staff members donate to get your first schoolwide play intervention started?
- What areas in your school need a makeover to be more trauma-informed?
- What are you totally pumped to change or design in your school? Explain why.

Gather your school leadership team, cabinet, or any other collaborative group and discuss your reflections on the content of this chapter.

5

The Mightiest Mindset Change

Making It Cool to Ask for and Get Help

Anything that is human is mentionable, and anything that is mentionable can be more manageable. When we talk about our feelings, they become less overwhelming, less upsetting, and less scary. The people we trust with that important talk can help us know that we are not alone.

—Fred Rogers—

Some of the most powerful work you can do as a school leader involves shifting the mindset students have when it comes to asking for help. The kids in your school need to know that there is a way for them to make their "big emotions" smaller and more manageable again, and that mastering this may require help from others. Ideally, you'll create a culture in which asking for help isn't just acceptable—it's actually cool.

In this chapter, we relate some real-life examples of how other school leaders have transformed their learning culture to make it easy and practical for both kids and adults to ask for and get help. We'll ask you to reflect on your own ability to own up to your mistakes and admit your wrongs—and will share examples of how we asked for help when we needed it. We will showcase one student's journey with trauma and how she has modeled for her peers what it looks like to ask for help, how to get help, and how to heal from trauma.

The Surprising Power of Vulnerability

Leaders often feel pressure to put on a stoic face and pretend that they are infallible, or immune to the possibility of making a mistake—especially a big mistake. But anyone who has held a leadership position knows that mistakes are part of the territory. In fact, mistakes and failures are foundational to innovation.

If it is generally understood that mistakes and failures are part of living and learning as adults, why is it so uncommon for students to see and hear educators talking about their errors and struggles? When adults in a school fail to talk about their mistakes they are encouraging kids to do the same. Not only is honesty the preferred approach, but it is also a terrific dynamic to promote learning. For example, a teacher asks for a quick "thumbs-up if you understand"

and sees smiles and thumbs pointing to the ceiling across the classroom—but how many of those positive responses are simply kids afraid to admit they are lost or don't understand (and think that everybody else does)?

Consider how this principle applies to the general social-emotional well-being of your students. As we have previously mentioned, a classroom procedure (fire drill, active-shooter drill), literature discussion (death of a character, tender exchange between parent and child), or something as random as teachers raising their voices at students can produce an emotional response for students who've experienced trauma. According to Sacks and Murphey (2018), "Just under half (45 percent) of children in the United States have experienced at least one ACE, which is similar to the rate of exposure found in a 2011–2012 survey. In Arkansas, the state with the highest prevalence, 56 percent of children have experienced at least one ACE" (p. 2). When students feel emotionally safe enough to share their rising anxiety, tension, or fears, you have created something amazing and beautiful in your school. You have established, through teaching and being vulnerable to model by your own example, a community of people who care for one another. This kind of learning equips students to thrive in school and in their lives beyond it.

Let's look at some ways to start this empowering mindset shift among your students.

▶ Be Authentic and Available

How authentic are you with your students? Take a moment to look at the question set in Figure 5.1 and capture some reflections.

We're sure you feel some level of pressure to conform to an external expectation of what you are "supposed" to be and do based

5.1 Reflection on Your Authenticity: Behaviors with Students

Focus Behavior	I do this a lot	I do this occasionally	I never do this
When I am having a bad day, I share with students that I am struggling.			
I share with students when I fail or doubt myself.			
I admit my mistakes, blunders, and bloopers in front of students.			
I talk with students about times when I needed and asked for help.			
I admit when I don't know the answer.			
I share with students stories of times when I have worked hard to overcome the odds.			
Notes			

on your official, and unofficial, roles. It's natural to strive to live up to those role expectations, but doing so to the degree that you completely sublimate your real self serves neither you nor your students. When you mask and hide your feelings, you teach kids that is how they should deal with trauma. By contrast, when kids see authentic adults who are open to sharing their own struggles, failures, shortcomings, and blemishes, they understand that these are "real people" who are also working through adversity to find wellness and success.

So the next time a student asks, "How're you today?" don't automatically reply that you are fine. Be honest. If it's been a tough week, it's OK to say that. Being authentic isn't sharing all of your life's problems; it's being upfront and letting kids know where you are emotionally at that moment.

Slowing Down for Self-Reflection and Greater Awareness

If you pause to consider how you are feeling and ponder what the underlying causes might be, you may be able to verbalize why you need help. Find time to meditate, pray, or simply be alone to reflect and pause. If your world is moving by at a rapid pace, it's even more important to be intentional in your self-care and to make sure you slow down. When you keep going, it's possible to become blinded to your true feelings—which may be suppressed in the effort of simply facing the next task ahead. Instead, schedule some time to slow down. Get in the pattern of going for a walk, use the Calm app to take a breath, or take some time to write about your feelings and life journey. By doing this, you model the importance of slowing down for students; this demonstrates the first step—getting in touch with their feelings—that will lead them to seek help when they need it.

Modeling How to Ask for Help

Failure will happen. One effective way to show your vulnerability, and also become more relatable and real, is to share some of your stories of failure—and the lessons that failing has taught you. Your failure stories model bravery for your students: they will learn that admitting mistakes, and examining failure, can also lead to incredible success.

Relate examples of failure from your own school experience as well as from the culture at large—but make sure you are telling the powerful stories of adults who benefitted from asking for help.

Although it may be tempting to share powerful, life-changing stories, resist that pull and find everyday examples that will help build a culture in which asking for help is the norm. This might be the "expert teacher" who asks a student for help with technology. It could be a principal who asks a teacher to explain a content skill or concept that's outside her own area of expertise. It could be one teacher asking another for help changing a tire, or the school nurse asking the counselor for a recommendation for an outside therapist. Recognizing that "no one is as smart as everyone" focuses on relying on one another's strengths and asking for the help others can provide.

Sharing real-life examples of adults needing and asking for help opens the door for students to feel comfortable doing the same. Consider holding a week where teachers share five different examples (one each day) from their lives about asking for help and reflect on how it worked out for them. If you've set the stage for sharing (i.e., your school is a safe and supportive space), teachers could then transition to a whole-class discussion where students also share their stories of needing to ask for help.

It's also essential to own your *current* mistakes. Don't cover them up or breeze over them. When a student points out an error, don't dismiss the student. Instead, capitalize on this opportunity to share how the mistake isn't fatal and that you've learned from it. Welcome feedback like this and embrace the opportunity to grow from failure. Following this approach empowers students to see failure as an opportunity to get better rather than an experience that's final.

Being Visible and Connected

There are days every week where Andrea spends time in the elementary school lunchroom. She moves like a bumblebee from table to table, sitting with students and talking with them about how school is going, what they're doing—all the while gauging *how* they are doing.

Are you standing at your school's front door in the mornings? Do you know your students' names and call to them as they enter the building? If not, you are missing a way to assess your students' demeanor as they begin their day. This simple gesture can make a big difference in building relationships; it also helps you keep track of how kids are doing on a daily basis.

Students need to see staff members who know them by name, take an interest in their lives, and are approachable. When you strategically position this type of staff member at all of the main entrances in the morning, you welcome students to school in a way that makes it easy for a student to ask for help and easy for a staff member to identify students who look like they might need help.

This visibility and ability to discern when a kid needs help remind Bill of his mom, who was always home when he got home from school, greeting him with a hug and asking about his day. But his mom knew how Bill's school day had gone as soon as she saw him walk through the door and could quickly assess if he was frustrated, upset, angry, or sad. Educators need to have this same keen ability. Educators who can assess a student's wellness by a simple observation will be able to take the next step of supporting students in getting the help they need.

▶ Make It Easy to Ask for Help

Use technology tools that allow students to share their need for help without forcing them to do it in the large-group, public sphere. This could be as simple as creating the expectation that you will be looking for email messages asking for help. If you use a learning management system (e.g., Schoology, Canvas, Google Classroom, BlackBoard), make sure students have ways to connect with teachers directly in addition to whole-class discussion boards. Apps like Remind, SeeSaw, and ClassDojo also can facilitate this kind of honest communication. When teachers mention (without using student names) that they routinely have class members asking for help using these channels of communication, it helps build a culture where asking is not only accepted but encouraged.

Bill and Dave's school district uses the Safe2Say app to allow students to report when they or some of their peers need help. Students download this app on their phone so they have it ready to use whenever they or a friend need assistance. Posters throughout the school highlight the app and provide regular reminders to students about how and when to use it.

Bill also has red SNAP (Student Needs Assistance Program) mailboxes throughout his school. Students are encouraged to drop notes in the boxes if they or a fellow student needs help. Students can drop an anonymous note and the school counseling team will follow up. These boxes are checked frequently to make sure kids who are in need get help right away. In Nebraska, our friends at Omaha Burke High School tell us that they are incorporating the Mood Meter in classrooms and doing emotional check-ins with students. They're looking into having the Mood Meter app installed on all student and teacher iPads so they can utilize this tool in their conversations.

▶ Gather (and Use!) Wellness Data

School leaders gather a great deal of academic achievement and growth data, and they should. However, do you also gather social-emotional and mental-health wellness data to make invisible traumatic experiences more visible? Consider having all your students and staff anonymously complete an adverse childhood experiences questionnaire. The one provided by the Center for Healthcare Strategies is an excellent resource (Schulman & Maul, 2019).

The National Alliance on Mental Illness (2022) has emphasized the importance of schools conducting regular mental health screenings of students, which "allow for early identification and intervention." Notably,

> approximately 50 percent of lifetime mental health conditions begin by age 14. At the same time, the average delay between when symptoms first appear and intervention is approximately 11 years. . . . Early treatment may also lessen long-term disability and prevent years of suffering. Health care screenings are common in this country, and mental health screenings should be no exception. (paras. 1–2)

Your school is constantly measuring and assessing the academic needs of students; how well are you assessing the students' social-emotional and mental health, and trauma? It is essential to invest just as much money, time, and resources in students' mental health as you do in their academic well-being.

Bill and Dave's school district uses a computer filtering system that provides principals with alerts any time a student types in something to their school-issued computer that could be potentially dangerous or unsafe. The principal is then able to identify whether students need to meet with a crisis counselor, who then follows up with students in need during school time. Outside school hours, the principal team members follow up and make the necessary contacts to help students access the support they need. These alerts have been key in identifying students who need help but would not reach out for it in the traditional setting. The alerts are sent to all tech team members and principals in the building. Having multiple eyes on the alerts makes sure nothing—or no one—is missed.

▶ Let Kids Inspire Other Kids

Provide opportunities for older students to share examples of how they asked for help and how it positively affected their lives. Peer tutoring programs at secondary schools and "study buddies" at elementary schools can channel the power of students mentoring students. Consider establishing student teams to support key transitions in students' lives at school—8th graders helping prepare 5th graders for the transition to middle school, upperclassmen supporting rising high school freshmen. Seniors can give freshmen a valuable peek into the "end of the story." Also try to connect kids who are willing to share their traumatic experiences and healing successes with others who find themselves in similar circumstances. Perhaps your school counselor could facilitate groups where kids can inspire one another, changing the trajectory of lives.

When Bill and Dave worked together at Pottsgrove High School in Pennsylvania, they were part of an inspiring kids-helping-kids effort that was initiated and led by a student, Sarah Pennington. The courage she displayed influenced hundreds of students—and placed her on a journey that has affected thousands more.

Sarah's experience of struggling with mental health is not unusual among high school students. In a *York Daily Record* Profile article, Ruland (2019) wrote that

> the thoughts about suicide would come in waves—never something Sarah Pennington had the intention to act on, but they were there, nonetheless. It was around this time that Sarah also started to lose her hair. First, her eyebrows disappeared, that's how her mother, Michelle Pennington, describes it. But then, the strawberry blonde locks on her head became scarce and the bald patches seemed to multiply. (para. 1)

Sarah has an impulse-control disorder called trichotillomania, which led to her pulling hair from her scalp. An inpatient treatment helped her develop coping mechanisms and empowered her; this young lady who initially was afraid to remove a headband or hat decided to show just how beautiful bald could be by entering the Miss Pennsylvania Pageant with her service dog, Daisy, at her side. Her participation raised awareness, and also created an audience eager to hear Sarah's story. Sarah realized her struggle, and story, could help others heal, too.

Sarah has refused to allow her disorder to define her as a person. Instead, she has worked to be a survivor who uses her experience to inspire others. During her junior year, Sarah met with Bill and asked if she could share her struggles with students in an assembly on the topic of mental health. At this time, she had been recognized nationally for her efforts in bringing awareness to mental health for students. Bill and Dave began to strategize what the event would look like.

To be honest, Bill and Dave were nervous about hosting a student-led assembly—especially one focused on mental health and led by a student. Isn't the school leadership team supposed to be responsible for any message students receive? Putting their fears aside, they opened the door—no, opened the *floodgates* to increase student voice in their school. Ever since then, Pottsgrove High School has been changed by the inspiring story and voice of one student, Sarah Pennington.

During the assembly, Sarah shared her personal struggle with mental health, showed pictures of herself during her darkest times, and shared how she is working every day to be a survivor. She listed warning signs for students, suggested ways to get help, and provided inspiration for other students to seek help when struggling with mental health challenges. The assembly and Sarah's message resulted in more students going to the school counseling office asking for help than any other assembly the school had had. Sarah worked with the school counselors to support students seeking help and worked alongside these students to encourage them to keep moving forward.

▶ Stress Personal Connection

In Chapter 3, we encouraged you to put relationships first. One way to do this is through the practice of *relationship mapping,* which is an intentional effort to connect students in need with caring adults in your school.

The elementary school where Andrea works has a program that pairs teachers with students, as a way to build community and support kids. Many of the teachers in the building have committed to connecting with a small group of students one-on-one at least once a week. Teachers play card games with students during recess, have lunch with them, or simply have a 5- to 10-minute conversation about how school is going. The goal of this specific program—and of all relationship mapping—is simple: fostering relationships.

These relationships can turn into opportunities for staff to share their stories with students, helping to develop a mindset or change old ways of thinking about mistakes, and build the understanding that asking for help is OK. Culture takes time to take shape, and it can only happen effectively with a plan and a commitment to see it through. Part of this commitment is being intentional. This starts from the top of your school organization all the way down. Everyone should view creating this atmosphere as a task that is just as important as the work they do around academic pursuits.

Building Smaller Communities

A few years ago, Andrea's school adopted a "house" system to further develop school culture. Students stay in the same house throughout their entire elementary school career, so they really get to know their house members. Houses consist of kids from every grade level, building a community across grades. Kids interact with other students they would have never otherwise had the opportunity to get to know. Community members design shirts each year for the houses; each house has their own name and color. Special house meetings and competitions (Color Wars and School Olympics) are held throughout the school year. At "house days" each month, students eat breakfast together and complete a task related to their house themes, which are based on important character traits. Houses earn points based on attendance and other school incentives, and monthly celebrations recognize the house with the most points: students line the halls to cheer for their classmates after morning assembly. This program has improved culture in one school in a huge way.

Providing Families with Strategic Support

A well-rounded trauma-informed program supports and collaborates with families. Doing this supports students and helps to strengthen their families.

Our friends at Pinewood Elementary School in Michigan are working to bridge the gap with families to provide additional support. This included hiring parent liaisons, to help create a bridge between the school and families and support any needs: "food insecurity, transportation, access to health care, access to winter clothes. The positions have made a big difference for some of our most needy families."

At Bill's school, a social worker helps families identify counseling services. This social worker also provides families with resources to support their efforts to deal with grief, manage mental health, and heal from trauma. Another possible approach to explore are home visit programs. Although they are often a way to forge home–school connections and celebrate student achievement, they might also be used to share resources and support options with families.

▶ Develop a Student Support System

Caring for kids means having a fluid social-emotional learning curriculum and embedding those components into school practices across all areas. These practices begin with your bus drivers and greeters and flow through those who teach in your school's classrooms and those who work in common areas. This extends to your after-school clubs, performance groups, and sports teams. Everyone should be trained on how to identify and help with kids' well-being. Imagine the difference if all staff in your district were trained in identifying students' needs. As an education leader, you must provide the training, follow-up, resources, and conditions for success in your culture and climate. Only then will these powerful practices permeate all aspects of your school.

As we mentioned in Chapter 1, however, students' mental health needs often cannot be addressed solely by in-school resources such as counselors and other trained staff. These individuals cannot be expected to carry the entire burden of the mental health needs of students; it's essential for schools to reach outside their doors for help and support.

A program at Rio Hondo High School in Texas provides telemedicine for students in the area of mental health assessments. Their principal, Asael Ruvalcaba, shared that we have partnered with UTRGV to offer the Texas Child Health Access Through Telemedicine (TCHATT) program. TCHATT connects children and adolescents with mental health services in the K-12 school system via telemedicine. This program has really helped and supported our students' mental health. (Personal communication, February 14, 2021)

At Bolivar High School in Missouri, licensed clinical therapists work with students on a weekly basis. According to their principal, "The work of the clinical therapist working with our students is one part of our comprehensive plan to support the mental health needs of students."

Offering Courses and Training on Mental Health

Many schools require students to take courses on financial literacy. Why not on mental health? Bolivar High School in Missouri offers a Foundations of Well-Being course where students learn strategies to support good mental health. At Bill's school, all students receive QPR (question, persuade, refer) suicide prevention training (https://qprinstitute.com) and Hope for Tomorrow education (http://www.hopetomorrow.org/about/). The QPR program educates students on how to support, get help, and work with others who might be considering suicide. Hope for Tomorrow is a program designed to help students with their mental and emotional well-being.

Providing Warm Welcomes

Boyertown West Middle School in Pennsylvania has a program called "Bear Ambassadors" designed to connect incoming 6th grade students with a positive peer group of older students in grades 7 and 8. These student ambassadors are trained to serve as leaders in the school and welcome new students. Even more important, they work to identify ways they can help and support their fellow classmates.

Programs like this make it easy to ask a peer for help in a way that's nonthreatening.

Many schools experience a fair amount of turnover in student population each year. Students move away, and students move in. At Pottsgrove Middle School, where Bill works, they recognized the importance of intentional transition events at the start of an academic year (e.g., 6th Grade Welcome Night, Freshman Orientation, Elementary Welcome Nights)—but also that these should not be one-and-done events. In order to help new students joining school midyear to feel more welcome (and to be more willing to ask for help), they are assigned a grade-level peer as their "tour guide" for their first six-day cycle of classes.

This tour guide student is an immediate, practical resource for questions like "What's the bell schedule?" or "Where's the nurse's office?"—but the larger purpose is to help every student feel like this is a school where it's always OK to ask for help. A wide range of students are always willing to serve as tour guides, helping the newest members feel welcome, and relationships that start as "assignments" often become authentic friendships as time progresses. It's a lesson worth reflecting on: when someone is vulnerable, and someone else listens and provides help, the connection between people can be powerful. For many students, being heard is not a common experience. Peer-to-peer programs like these help build a culture of communication and support across your entire school.

Building Trust

Bill's school also has a program designed to make it easier for students to establish secure connections with trusted sources of help. It's called Unity Day, and it connects grade-level teams of students with peers, teachers, and school counselors in a way that nurtures a caring community that prioritizes listening to, and really hearing, one another.

The first Unity Day was created almost 20 years ago with the help of Thom Stecher and Associates. Student experiences were designed to align with the Collaborative for Academic, Social, and Emotional Learning (CASEL) tenets (2021). Focusing on the CASEL competencies—self-awareness, self-management, social awareness, relationship skills, and responsibility decision making—helps the school staff increase student success, both academically and in their general well-being. Instead of a schoolwide assembly program, Unity Days are team-based, day-long experiences that engage students both physically and emotionally. Figure 5.2 provides an overview of what they are all about.

5.2 Overview of Unity Day

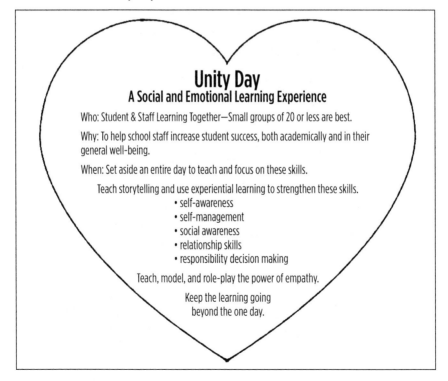

Unity Day
A Social and Emotional Learning Experience

Who: Student & Staff Learning Together—Small groups of 20 or less are best.

Why: To help school staff increase student success, both academically and in their general well-being.

When: Set aside an entire day to teach and focus on these skills.

Teach storytelling and use experiential learning to strengthen these skills.
- self-awareness
- self-management
- social awareness
- relationship skills
- responsibility decision making

Teach, model, and role-play the power of empathy.

Keep the learning going beyond the one day.

👥 Reflecting on a Help- Seeking Mindset Change

Teaching students to know how, when, and where to ask for help is paramount in the healing process. Consider these questions:

- What are the biggest barriers keeping your students, or your staff, from seeking out the help they need at school?
- Where do you stand on the five strategies for motivating students affected by trauma to seek help—being authentic and available, making it easy to ask for help, using wellness data, using peer supports and examples, and having an overarching support system?
- If you feel one of these areas is a great need at your school, what steps will you take to implement the strategy?
- When a need arises for help that extends beyond your school resources, is there a clear path in place to provide it? Do faculty and staff know the process? What needs to happen to establish or communicate this work more clearly?

Gather your school leadership team, cabinet, or any other collaborative group and discuss your reflections on the content of this chapter.

Treatment
for Trauma

Caring for Kids in Ways That
Support Learning and Growth

*The difference between making a judgment
and having empathy is understanding the story.*

—Thomas C. Murray—
Personal & Authentic

In this chapter, we focus on research-based, practical, and easy-to-implement strategies school leaders can use to help students who are experiencing trauma. We also showcase real-life examples of

leaders who are supporting students affected by trauma and helping them find success. As with the content of preceding chapters, we
encourage you to reflect on your own practice and identify areas in
which you need to stretch and grow to better support students who
are experiencing trauma.

Bill will never forget the day a student ran into his office shouting that a teacher needed his immediate help: a classmate was crying uncontrollably in the back of a classroom, and the teacher didn't
know what was going on or what to do. After moving the rest of the
students to another classroom, Bill walked to the back of the room to
talk with the crying student, who we'll call Anthony. He learned that
one of Anthony's parents had died by suicide earlier in the day, and
the boy had heard about it from a Facebook post. While the assistant
principal reached out to the surviving parent and arranged for the
student to be picked up, Bill, a member of the school's counseling
team, and a school resource officer sat in the room, providing tis-
sues, water, and quiet support. Bill will never forget how the sleeve
of his suit-jacket sleeve was soaked from Anthony's tears.

The support provided by Bill's school did not stop at the end
of that traumatic day. The counseling team surrounded Anthony's family with support, resources, care, and love. The entire staff
embraced the family through their darkest days and worked to support them. Weeks after the incident, the school counselors would
follow up, connect, and express their care for Anthony. They worked
to connect the family with grief counselors, ran errands, and were
constantly checking in to make sure Anthony was doing as well as
he could. The student's team of teachers surrounded and supported
him emotionally and academically, making accommodations to
support his learning, adjusting timelines to help him ease back into
school, and excusing him from assignments missed. These teachers
understood that Anthony's trauma far outweighed the expectations

in their class, and they made the necessary adjustments to support his learning. The student resumed a full course load when he was ready, guided by counselors who were in consultation with the remaining parent. The counselors also partnered closely with the teachers so that Anthony's transition to a regular workload was a team effort, and his social and emotional health was monitored.

It took a schoolwide team effort—school counselors, social workers, crisis counselor, teachers, and principals—to fully support Anthony and help him to get back on his feet. Teamwork is foundational to support students in their learning, especially those students impacted by trauma.

The Effects of Trauma on Students

The American Society for the Positive Care of Children (2021) advocates for a future where all children can live happy, healthy, and productive lives. In Chapter 1, we encouraged you to be aware of students' adverse childhood experiences (ACEs). Here are some sobering statistics collected and reported by the American Society for the Positive Care of Children and data from research on ACEs:

- In the United States, 146,706 children receive foster care services.
- Almost five children die each day from child abuse.
- Annually, almost 65,000 children are sexually abused.
- Children who experience child abuse and neglect are nine times more likely to become involved in criminal activity.
- Five of the 10 top causes of death are associated with ACEs.
- Preventing ACEs could reduce the number of adults with depression by as much as 44 percent.
- Preventing ACEs could prevent up to 2.5 million cases of overweight/obesity.

Repeated exposure to abuse, neglect, transiency, violence, and other forms of trauma contribute to both learning and behavioral problems. These issues present a variety of obstacles to learning, including social-emotional challenges—trouble forming relationships, disconnect from learning, struggle in relating to peers productively, anxiety, inability to self-regulate emotions—and learning challenges such as executive functioning deficits or difficulty focusing on assignments.

But there is hope: If you can nurture and design a learning culture that supports students affected by trauma, you will free them to thrive in the classroom and life. This, in turn, enables you to provide them with the skills they need to be successful in their adult lives. As we stressed in Chapter 3, the best learning takes place within caring relationships; your work is to build positive, caring, and supportive relationships with students. Doing so will increase your success in reaching them as learners.

▶ Connect Every Student with a Caring Adult

According to the Harvard Graduate School of Education (2021) and its Making Caring Common Project,

> there may be nothing more important in a child's life than a positive and stable relationship with a caring adult. For students, a positive connection to at least one school adult—whether a teacher, counselor, sports coach, or other school staff member—can have tremendous benefits that include reduced bullying, lower dropout rates, and improved social emotional capacities. (para. 1)

Bill recalls one of his teachers playing football with kids on the West Pottsgrove Elementary School playground. The teacher served as the "steady quarterback," but he was so much more than that. He was a caring adult that the kids looked up to—and someone the kids knew they could go to for help. His availability on the playground communicated that he cared and was there to support them. Bill can still remember the teacher saying, "Ziggy, go straight out and do a button hook and be ready, because the ball is coming to you." As the teacher called the plays, he demonstrated his belief in kids—Bill was convinced that he could catch the pass and felt at that moment like an NFL All-Star. Even more important, when he dropped the ball (and he did that often), the teacher would say "shake it off and expect the ball next time around." Some of Bill's friends who had experienced trauma saw that teacher as the father they didn't have, and that support system was a pillar of strength in the school. He made students believe they could do things bigger than they ever imagined.

Trauma-affected students have more relationship challenges to sift through than most of their peers. Justin has seen at the elementary school level, where students are learning for the first time to develop the skills necessary for healthy relationships, the need for mentoring and modeling. For many of these students, a connection with a positive adult role model is the first step. If they are not learning what healthy relationships look like in school, they might not be learning it anywhere. Trauma-affected students in many cases have harmful, abusive relationships outside school and show up daily without the emotional tools they need to deal with their feelings. Taking the time and making the purposeful effort to create relationships between students and adults in your school is worth the effort, just as important as any academic intervention that you put into place.

The following are some strategies that will help you make sure that every child is connected to a caring adult in the school.

Relationship Mapping

In Chapter 5, we introduced you to relationship mapping, an intentional approach to connect students in need with caring adults in your school. Materials created by the Harvard Graduate School of Education (2021) as part of its Making Caring Common Project include lesson plans with a strategy for relationship mapping. The first step is to identify youth who do not currently have positive connections with school adults. Appropriate mentors are matched to these students; in addition to supporting the students, "mentors support one another through the successes and challenges of building relationships with students" (para 3).

Relationship mapping ensures that every student is known by at least one adult. Andrea's school started this practice during weekly professional learning community (PLC) meetings, and, very quickly, it was easy to see which of the students at school already had a strong network of support from staff and who needed more support. It was very eye-opening, in fact, to see that some students had several adults who felt a strong connection to them—through class, extracurricular activities, or community events—and that other kids may have had only one adult who had a connection to them.

The next step in that process is to be intentional about building relationships with those students so that they understand that they have several adults they can relate to on a daily basis. At Andrea's school, they realized that the students who had few connections were also more likely to have experienced trauma throughout their lives. Intentional relationship building helps all students, but especially those who have experienced trauma.

Justin offers the example of the Bulldog Lunch program (named after the school mascot) at Shiloh Hills Elementary School, which was designed so that participating teachers could regularly eat lunch and build relationships with one or two individual students that they didn't know very well previously. Part of the goal of this program was to have students come to see the adults in the building as real people who really cared about them. During Bulldog Lunches, teachers would play games and color with students, tell jokes, and just talk. There was no lesson plan, no structure. Connection and community are very important in helping students who are struggling. The best way to show kids you care for them is through your actions.

The Dot Project

At his school, Bill uses the "Dot Project" with faculty and staff to identify kids who need to be connected to a caring adult (Ginsburg, 2015; see Figure 6.1). They have found this activity to be a powerful way to ensure that every child is connected to someone who believes in them. This is key when working with students who are affected by trauma.

6.1 Ginsburg's Dot Project Process

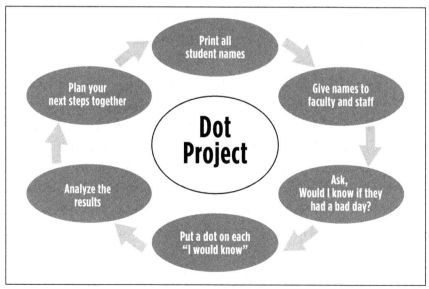

Source: Ginsburg, 2015.

The project begins with faculty and staff reviewing a student roster and asking themselves whether they would be able to know if each student listed was having a bad day. If they can answer with a resounding "Yes," they place a dot after the student's name. Students whose names feature few or no dots are flagged as being at risk: no one on staff knows them deeply. Staff members are encouraged to make stronger connections with these dot-less students: to welcome them, encourage them, push them, and connect them to the larger learning community.

Share pictures of the students at risk at your school with staff members, and encourage everyone to learn more about these young lives. Dots can be key data for an advisory program, guidance staff, mentoring initiative, interdisciplinary team, or extracurricular staff to use in their work with students at all grade levels. Everyone needs to be connected in order to succeed (Ziegler & Ramage, 2017).

Daily Check-ins

Students can often mask the trauma that hovers over their lives so that educators, even those closest to them, will never see it. This is why it's mission-critical to have a system of daily check-ins with students that you know have experienced trauma. These daily check-ins with a caring adult can go a long way in building a relationship, identifying changes in behavior, and providing support as needed.

When Dave and Bill worked together at a middle school, a number of staff members volunteered to check in each day with a group of students we knew were fragile, many of whom had experienced trauma. The daily checks-ins became key in helping these students find success in learning, and we identified some key elements that make this type of program work.

Accept adult volunteers. Don't force anyone to do this. You want willing, highly relational, and cooperative adults who see this as a mission to help kids rather than a duty assigned by their prin-cipal. And the adults who participate in this program don't need to all be teachers; they need to be the strongest relationship builders in your school. Consider involving paraeducators, custodians, secre-taries, and other support staff. The important thing is that everyone needs to be committed, and the check-ins are daily and regular. They can't be sporadic or infrequent.

Incorporate different ways of communicating. The adult and student could have a code such as a high-five means all is good, and a low-five (think of it as a high-five but where your hands natu-rally rest) says "I am struggling today." This will allow the adult to communicate with the student in a hallway full of students and still know how they are doing. Obviously, talking it out is always great—but so is a written check-in. Differentiate how your adult volunteers connect with kids.

Document and track. It's important to track the findings from daily check-ins to see how the students develop over a period of time. Communication between school personnel such as administra-tion, school counseling, faculty, paraeducators, and even parent volunteers can be a crucial way to track student progress to identify goals, supports, and interventions needed. Consider tracking this information through your school's Student Information System to allow for a universal approach to entering and viewing this data. By doing this, you allow the adults in the school to view the progress that can be shared at parent meetings, counseling sessions, or prog-ress reports.

▶ Focus on Mindfulness

In Chapter 4, we encouraged you to consider ways to encourage stu-dents to practice mindfulness, as they build their skills in self-care and self-management. The need to remain calm and focused is especially important for students affected by trauma; it helps them get to an emotional state in which they are ready to learn. Anxiety stands in the way of learning. Mindfulness can help break down those barriers and ready students for the learning ahead.

Monday Morning Mindfulness

When Dave was a middle school principal, one of his social studies teachers started her week with a "Monday morning mindfulness" activity for students. This 5- to 10-minute pause helps students focus and put aside any distractions or anxieties they have brought with them to the classroom. One Monday, this teacher took advantage of a snowy day and asked her students to look out the window and identify the farthest thing they could see. She then had them share their observations with classmates. Next, she asked them to focus on the closest thing they could see outside and share with their classmates. The entire time she was calmly reminding students that everyone needs to take advantage of what is in front of them right now, and modeled for them how to stay in the moment and work to put aside distractions—in short, how to be ready for learning.

Mindfulness Strategies

Dave's students practice mindfulness every week as part of the school's SEL focus, and many teachers have begun practicing these strategies throughout the week as well. Mindfulness strategies are proven and effective tools in working with students and in helping to address various barriers such as anxiety, frustration, and also self-esteem. The Mayo Clinic provides an excellent review on the importance of mindfulness along with some practical strategies to practice it in your school (Sparks, 2018). When doing check-ins with students, teachers also discuss mindfulness strategies; this strengthens students' use of these tools in coping with situations when they are by themselves. The Calm app and GoNoodle are both great digital tools for accessing mindfulness resources.

Teachers Take 10

At Andrea's elementary school, they recently inaugurated "Teachers Take 10." Teachers in the school can call and ask an administrator to come to the class and give them a break for a few minutes. Maybe it's been a particularly stressful day, or they just need a minute to get their thoughts together. The administrator will come to the classroom and continue with the lesson; teachers can go to the school's "calming corner" and just take a moment to improve their mental state. The calming corner has resources (e.g., fidget toys, coloring books, bubble timers, sketch pads) students and teachers can access. It's amazing what just a few minutes to decompress can do for someone's mental health.

▶ Build On-Ramps for Students

Author Andratesha Fritzgerald (2020) works tirelessly to help educators put antiracism and equity strategies into practice. She reminds us that sometimes well-intended interventions to help students can lead to frustration. Rather than express this frustration, the students "stall out." This metaphor of moving along a highway of learning and success leads to her urging educators to create the on-ramps that students need to access the highway. However, learners can get frustrated when educators focus entirely on the achievement data, isolate a gap in a skill or concept, and bring repeated instruction to that one area again and again. Anyone who is repeatedly confronted with their "weakest" area can easily grow weary, depressed, lethargic, or even confrontational. Some stalled students continue to sit patiently and quietly; others demand a different kind of intervention. Minority populations are especially at risk for stalling and becoming disproportionately represented as the lowest-achieving students. How much support does your school provide to students at risk of stalling? Or, as Fritzgerald asks, are you "more readily offering the promise of learning or the danger of failing for our brilliant Black and Brown students?" (p. 24).

Often, what stands in the way of students' access to learning is not a lack of strategic intervention but a lack of relationship. You must dedicate the time, despite perceived "loss of instruction," to ensure you are treating your students as people first and learners second. One of the best ways to honor students in this lifelong process of learning and growing is to acknowledge that you, their teachers, and students are in this learning process together. It's a great feeling to believe that one has been truly heard and truly understood. It's also powerful for students to realize that they, too, can teach their teachers.

This is more than "the student becoming the master." We're talking about continual, small moments of connectedness, such as when a digital-native student shares a technology fix for the Boomer-generation teacher or more fully explains the effect of life circumstances outside the classroom. When students feel safe enough and trust enough to unpack their "invisible backpack," they are teaching their teachers about themselves. Each child's invisible backpack holds worries, fears, past experiences, past trauma—everything else they're bringing to school with them that can present challenges to their engagement with traditional school settings and practices.

The "backpack" of an 8th grader at Bill and Dave's school (we'll call her Amiyah) included the responsibility of caring for three younger siblings every day after school. Preparing dinner, reading to her sisters and brother, and helping them get ready for bed made the prospect of Amiyah routinely completing homework or studying for quizzes and tests very unlikely.

Could her failure to complete homework and study be perceived as irresponsible? Could Amiyah herself be viewed as apathetic, unmotivated, and lacking organizational or time management skills? Could her tendency to fall asleep in class be interpreted as "not caring" about her education? Too often, this is exactly what is assumed. The reality is this young woman is demonstrating responsibility, time management, caring, and dedication beyond her years—but it remains in her backpack, and her story may never be known. Her mother may routinely reinforce the high value and life-changing power of education to rise above the struggles of generational poverty. Then Amiyah's teachers and aides chide her for not caring about school. Paying attention to the social-emotional life of any child, and being attuned with their general well-being, is a powerful antidote to the challenges any invisible backpack may contain.

▶ Establish Clear Routines

We have seen the benefits of classrooms where clear expectations and routines have been established, and rehearsed, to the point where they are embedded habits in the learning community. Clear routines help students arriving at your door to know what to expect and avoid the rising tension that often accompanies "surprises" for students with trauma. Instead of routine for routine's sake, consider routines that also help to build relationships.

Routines provide the structure and discipline that help a student working through trauma to thrive, a framework, and a safe place for learning. Some students don't have routines at home, which means they always live in a world of flux.

Greet Students and Staff Every Day

Some teachers line up students in the hallway, greeting each one intentionally as they enter the classroom. Others greet students as they trickle into the room from their previous location. These strategies are vital; all of your teachers should engage in daily greetings. As a school leader, you should also engage in this kind of personalization. It is harder to know every student when you are leading a school, but greeting students as they exit their morning buses sends a strong signal that you care about them as people. Greet students as you can, but greet every teacher every day. You might consider a morning routine that starts with "bus hellos" and then leads to a quick walk around your building to greet every teacher in their classroom. In the "olden days," a principal could hang around the faculty mailboxes and see teachers as they arrived and picked up their daily bulletin. Electronic communication has greatly improved the daily bulletin, but it has also decentralized a lot of the morning routines in schools. Be intentional about stopping into every classroom at some point during your day.

Routines that are common in elementary schools can also be effective practices in secondary schools. Sometimes a little tweak is all that's needed. For example, kindergarten students' three choices when greeting their teacher—"hello, high-five, or hug"—is not recommended for middle school or high school classrooms. But "hello, high-five, or heads-up" may be just the corny icebreaker that a student secretly welcomes because it means receiving individual attention every day from the teacher. In this case, "heads-up" is an invitation for students to honestly share that they are struggling to engage that day. The reason may be shared, or the reason may remain unspoken, but the teacher immediately knows the student is in a fragile place. Every day offers the opportunity for learners to deepen their relationship with their teachers. In Chapter 1, we encouraged you to be real and authentic; in Chapter 5, we talked about modeling asking for help. Talk to your teachers about incorporating this into their morning greetings and discussions with students. A simple statement like, "As we get started today, I want to let you all know I'm in a high-five mood!" or "I want to share a quick heads-up: I may appear a little distracted today because my daughter was sick this morning and I'm waiting to hear about her doctor appointment."

Assign Roles and Responsibilities

One way to capture the attention of students and instill responsibility and a sense of routine is to assign student jobs or responsibilities. When a student is responsible for handing out papers, watering the plants, feeding the fish, or helping to lead the bell-ringer activity, they become empowered for learning. Teachers, regardless of grade level or content area, can create a regular roster of jobs that students rotate into and out of. This routine develops responsibility and demonstrates to students that their teachers trust them to take the lead.

Trust students to do this work with fidelity and accuracy. Teach them what to do, model what you want to see, and set them free to get the job or task complete.

> If you see that a student hasn't completed their job, don't leap in and do it for them. When you do this, you're showing them that you don't trust that they can do it on their own. Instead, be patient and give them some time. (Cox, 2021, para. 3)

Teacher "10 and Two"

In the "10 and two" student engagement strategy, a teacher talks for no more than 10 minutes before giving students a chance to talk to each other for at least two minutes—a useful approach for many lessons. We'd like you to consider a variation that can help build stronger connections with your staff. Identify three or four staff members with whom you'll spend two minutes in conversation for 10 school days in a row. Get to know them as people, not just as employees. You will be amazed at how effective these short interactions become. Talking with five teachers will take only 10 minutes of conversation each day. Even with a large staff, you can spend two minutes with several people a day, in 10-day cycles, and reach your entire professional staff efficiently. (If you have 100 staff members, this might be a project for your administrative team.)

▶ Give Students Voice and Choice

In what ways can you strengthen student advocacy through promoting voice and choice in your school? The simple act of releasing power and control goes a long way in building authentic relationships. When you relinquish control, you exhibit trust in your students. This can be embedded in academic requirements by offering several assessment options for students to show what they know. It can be woven through many other aspects of the classrooms in your school—how student groups are formed, the rules for the classroom and school learning community, where students sit, which menu-board options they choose to get the points they need, how they take notes. The only nonnegotiable is that everyone participates in the learning community together. When students are given choice, they are empowered to thrive in a nurturing learning culture.

It's time to empower students to make their voice and choice heard in their schools, their communities, and the world; the future of civilization depends on it (Ziegler & Ramage, 2020). More important, allowing students to have voice and choice in their learning builds confidence and learning readiness in students affected by trauma—and, in turn, their learning is deepened and strengthened. Voice and choice provide students with the opportunity to learn in a way that gives them the autonomy to thrive, not just in the classroom but the world. Often, the voice and choice of students who experience trauma are suppressed by abusive adults, diminishing their feelings and thoughts. In our experience, empowering students to use their voice and exercise choice strengthens both their decision-making skills and leadership abilities and deepens their learning.

Choice in Assignment and Assessment

Be a school leader who fights for multiple ways, in every classroom, for students to show what they know. Don't allow your teachers to implement a one-size-fits-all approach to assessment. Implement grading practices and policies that ensure teachers offer multiple ways for students to complete your school's common formative assessments. Students benefit from the ability to choose what type of assignment or assessment they want to complete. Being able to choose from a variety of topics strengthens their level of engagement and interest in the learning. Choice in selecting a type of assessment may be a new thing for you, but we encourage you to try it. There are so many creative ways that students can demonstrate their knowledge and skills: creating a video, writing a blog, recording a podcast, designing a website, or acting out what they learned in a short play. When educators are willing to move away from the pen and paper of learning, students are given the ability to express their talents and giftedness.

Student Feedback

Be a leader who solicits student feedback on how to improve your school. Bill and his principal team meet regularly with students to gather feedback using the four questions in Figure 6.2. The trends in student responses guide decision making surrounding improvements in reaching and supporting all students.

These four simple questions, asked of four students from each grade level in your school, can help your work to transform learning and empower students. It's important to listen to what students say and act on their ideas to assure them that their voice really does make a difference. Students who have experienced trauma will feel supported when their ideas are listened to, implemented, and

6.2 Student Feedback Questions and Analysis

Questions	Sample Student Responses	Analysis
What does our school do really well?	• Teachers are great and really care about us. • Extracurricular programs are excellent, and there are lots of ways to stay involved. • School provides technology to help us find success. • Administrators and teachers listen to us.	*Students seem to feel staff's genuine investment and care. Our work to expand and promote afterschool activities is paying off.*
How could our school be better?	• Put paper towel dispensers in the bathrooms. Blow dryers aren't enough! • Add hot sauce in the cafeteria. And add a salad bar for more healthy food choices! • Expand the "excused" window for tardy students during inclement weather.	*Reminders that the state of the physical plant and the noninstructional experiences in school matter. Students are highly attuned to fairness.*
What do you dream our school could be?	• Can we get a swimming pool? • Win a state championship in every sport! • Have Wednesdays off!	*These dreams are of luxury, success, and ease. Important to know that students value these, but we might do more to get them thinking about learning-related visions. . . .*
What can you personally do to make our school a better place?	• Be a nicer person to other people. • Help fellow students who are struggling. • Be a good student, follow the rules, be kind, work hard, and do my best.	*Great that students see kindness and mutual support as key to our school's success. Let's investigate ways we might formalize this interest (a peer support program)?*

carried through to better their classrooms and school. It gives them a sense of ownership in their learning and school culture.

One of Bill's feedback sessions with students identified a trend: students wanted to be able to choose where they sat in the classroom or what group they worked with. We understand that this may not be accomplished all of the time. The teachers at Bill's school, however, provide some choice in these two key areas. As we discussed in Chapter 4, there are alternatives to traditional classroom design (i.e., students sitting in rows, on hard chairs, uncomfortable desks). How different might students' interactions and learning be if they had other options—some high-top tables and flexible seating areas, somewhere in the school? Implementing small changes such as these, drawn from student voice and feedback, is not only the task of a teacher, but something you as a school leader should support.

▶ Build in Safeguards

Intentionally focusing on relationship building reflects sensitivity to students who may bring deeper issues than are easily addressed in the classroom setting. As part of your relationship building with students, you may uncover serious issues. Other times, when consistent opportunities to build an appropriate relationship with a student have been completely stonewalled, you may suspect a larger issue is contributing. In Chapter 5, we stressed the importance of developing a student support system. Your team includes teachers, school counselors, social workers, building administrators, and other professionals; everyone needs to communicate and work together to ensure that students are connected with the mental health resources they need.

We have also mentioned how important it is to recognize when it's time to tag-team and bring in resources that can supplement your training and expertise. One of the best ways to accomplish this is to build safeguards into your whole system. In Chapter 5, we mentioned systems (e.g., Safe2Say) that allow students to anonymously alert school officials about peers who might be in physical or mental health danger. Such alerts can be a phone call or text message that is delivered to key personnel at the school and district level. Immediate needs (e.g., suicide ideation) may also be delivered directly to local police so a well-check can be conducted 24 hours a day. Some school administrators we know have created an anonymous tip line in-house to accomplish the same kind of support and intervention.

Artificial intelligence can also be part of your systemwide support offering; there are programs (e.g., Gaggle, Social Sentinel) that monitor electronic documents sent among and between students and teachers, or public social media posts. These AI programs can help identify dangerous or life-threatening information sent in the invisible space of digital traffic and alert you, so you can connect with students and families who may be on the edge of a tragedy. The alerts that are not life-threatening will also point you toward opportunities to care for students and families. Discovering relationships that are trending toward fighting or violence, stepping into acts of bullying and discrimination, finding relationships that are bordering on abuse, or being alerted to an individual student's cry for help are all opportunities to care for fragile students and demonstrate concern for and commitment to them.

👥 Reflecting on Treating Trauma

K–12 educators can make a real difference in the lives of the students with whom they interact. Ludy-Dobson and Perry (2010) considered the power of relationships and emphasized the following:

We expect "therapy"—healing—to take place in the child via epi-
sodic shallow relational interactions with highly educated but
poorly nurturing strangers. We undervalue the powerful therapeutic impact of a caring teacher, coach, neighbor, grandparent,
and a host of other potential "co-therapists." (p. 18)

As you work toward building a trauma-informed culture at
your school to care for students and support their learning, take a
moment to reflect and identify areas where you need to improve:

- Do you help adults in your school gain skills for building rela-
  tionships with students?
- Are the adults in your school able to identify signs of trauma?
- Does every student in your school have a connection with a
  caring adult there?
- Do you and your teachers check in with students on a daily
  basis?
- Do your at-risk students have "on-ramps" to the education
  highway?
- Do students in your school have voice and choice?
- What challenged your thinking the most in the chapter?
  Why?

Gather your grade-level partners, school leadership team, cabinet, or any other collaborative group and discuss your reflections on
the content of this chapter.

7

Secondary Trauma

Caring for Staff Members

Secondary traumatic stress is sort of the consequence
of being a good teacher. If you care about your students,
you're probably not going to avoid it.

Jessica Lander, teacher

Listening to students tell their story of trauma or supporting students through trauma can have lasting effects on adults. Providing professional learning on secondary trauma is key to helping staff through the difficult job of supporting students in and through trauma. As a leader, you must ensure that the adults in your school are taking care of themselves, having their needs met, and are not alone in the journey. In this chapter, we provide some proven strategies to address secondary trauma with staff—strategies that will help them work through restoration—and ideas for moving faculty and staff forward as they work with students affected by trauma. Stories of leaders who are making a difference will inspire and inform your own work and rekindle your call to elevate students to the work they can do right now in your school—and in their lives.

Bill has personal experience with secondary trauma affecting his job and life. He was working with a student who experienced a horrific violent trauma and the loss of a family member—and the family wanted to talk about the experience, share gruesome details, and go over how things happened. Bill also needed to work with local law enforcement to better support the family. During a call with the police investigators, they too painted a horrific picture of the event.

Bill just could not shake out of his mind what he had heard, and he kept seeing it taking place, over and over again. He became depressed and withdrawn, saddened by the events. The experience had rattled everyone in the school, students and staff—and Bill needed to be strong during the day to lead and support them. After a counselor from the county office visited the school and talked with faculty and staff about grief and how to work through it, Bill called his leadership mentor and discussed his secondary trauma and grief. With the help of his mentor, Bill was able to work through it and have a better perspective on how to move forward. Bill's wife, a nurse, is used to dealing with secondary trauma, and she also offered ideas for healing and moving forward. More important, she was a caring listener, allowing Bill to cry, talk, and share his honest feelings about the pain he was experiencing. With these supports, Bill was supported in the healing process.

Secondary Trauma and Teacher Attrition

The stress that comes with caring for students and being exposed to secondary trauma can be overwhelming and debilitating. Morrison (2019) has noted that "more teachers are dropping out after their first year than at any time in the last 20 years, while one in three leave after five years" (para. 2), and over "44 percent of new teachers leave the profession within the first five years" (Ingersoll et al., 2018, para. 8). High school teachers are most likely to seek employment elsewhere, "with 61 percent saying they have thought about leaving the profession" (Hess, 2019, p. 7).

The stress and anxiety mentioned in these reports are often related to secondary trauma. Secondary trauma can mask itself as stress, burnout, or anxiety.

What Is Secondary Trauma?

Secondary trauma is the emotional spillover or residue of exposure that teachers and other helping professionals have from working with people who have suffered or are suffering from trauma. Listening to such stories in effect makes them witnesses to some of the pain, heartache, fear, and terror that traumatized individuals have experienced. Many teachers can recall sad or painful experiences that their students have shared. Over time, this takes a toll, regardless of one's efforts to avoid being affected. School leaders must have ways to address secondary trauma among teachers, an intentional plan to support them. As society changes in many ways, the stress level that both teachers and students face is increasing—and affects both how students learn and how educators approach their job.

Secondary trauma is real; it permeates the lives of educators (Baicker, 2020). Any traumatic experiences educators may have gone through can resurface, weighing them down and preventing them from moving forward. Karen Baicker (2020), executive director of the Yale Child Study Center, noted that "despite schools making great strides implementing a trauma-informed approach to caring for students, the emotional distress that educators experience when working with traumatized students is still widely overlooked" (para. 4). Things need to be done differently in education. It's time to act in ways that address the spillover of trauma. School and district leaders need to provide support, education, and options for educators experiencing secondary trauma.

Educators use several terms for secondary trauma, including "compassion fatigue" and "empathic distress" (Alber, 2018). Alber observed that "for teachers, that feeling of deep empathy for a student, coupled with knowing that you've done all you can do—and the child is still perhaps still suffering—can cause considerable distress" (para. 5). Baicker (2020) described a type of stress that results from helping or wanting to help those who are traumatized or under significant emotional duress, relating the experience of a 4th grade teacher in New Orleans who saw trauma spilling into her own life. The teacher, Sarah, said, "This year already, I've had a student whose parent was killed, and others whose parents are in and out of jail. I've had to confiscate a weapon. Some of my kids are homeless." Sarah does her best to help her students, including greeting them at the door with hugs and helping them get counseling. But at the end of the day, as she tries to fall asleep, "she finds herself worrying about the difficulties her kids may be facing at that very moment" (para. 1). Baicker reminds us that over half of all children in the United States suffer from some kind of trauma—and teachers recognize that helping children cope with outside challenges is part and parcel with helping them learn. But she also points out that we know a lot less about the effect that student trauma has on educators, and we do a lot less to help *them* cope.

Empathic distress is the opposite extreme of the empathy gap Hattie talked about when discussing teachers who are not effective in building relationships with students. These teachers fail to be able to place themselves in their student's shoes (Hattie & Yates, 2014). We have seen far more teachers who dive in, relate to their students, and often take on a great deal of empathy. This is the situation Alber (2018) observed as empathic distress.

Indicators of Secondary Trauma in Adults

"When psychologists put themselves in their clients' shoes through their use of therapeutic empathy, they 'taste' the same emotional and physiological 'pain' of their clients" (Diehm & Roland, 2015, para. 2). Teachers often experience a similar phenomenon as they absorb the trauma their students bring to the classroom. Secondary trauma can often mask itself as certain feelings and emotions:

- Increased anxiety
- Sunday anxiety (dreading the return to school on Monday)
- Loss of confidence in one's abilities as an educator
- Feelings of sadness, depression, or hopelessness
- Physical and mental exhaustion
- Lethargy or loss of energy
- Desire to isolate and be alone
- Difficulty concentrating, focusing, and making decisions
- Loss of appetite or binge eating
- Increased alcohol consumption
- Overmedicating
- Desire to leave the profession of education

The teacher who leaves school exhausted, frustrated, and stressed out may write it off as a hard day at work—but this could actually reflect the emotional toll that secondary trauma takes. The resilient nature of educators often prevents them from recognizing the secondary trauma that is negatively affecting their lives. They will work to bounce back, get over it, carry on, put it behind them, or simply try to ignore it, hoping it will go away rather than facing it for what it is. Secondary trauma sneaks up like a lion waiting to pounce on its prey—or it can hit hard, like being run over by a charging bull. Secondary trauma can weigh a teacher down slowly, as rocks and bricks fill an invisible backpack that eventually will prevent moving forward. There are ways, however, that school leaders can care for teachers affected by students' trauma.

▶ Develop a Secondary Trauma Action Plan

For true growth to take place, the school leader must have a strategic plan focused on supporting teachers through secondary trauma. This plan must be practical, relevant, and sustainable, not something that is dusted off in the midst of a traumatic experience. Just the opposite: this needs to be a living document that is regularly refreshed and reflected upon.

To really make a difference, this should be a districtwide effort, with a committee devoted to investing the time and energy needed to address staff needs. However, this can also be a solo effort, by you, for your school and its staff. The first step is to identify some of the common deficiencies or problems that staff members face when it comes to trauma, stress, and burnout. The next step is to formulate a coherent plan, with input from staff into how, specifically, to address these issues. All levels of staff should be included in the design, development, and implementation of the plan. Teachers and staff who are working to be more aware of their feelings, stress levels, and understanding how secondary trauma affects them and their performance benefit everyone.

This plan should be embedded from the first day of school, the first hire, or the first professional learning program focused on self-care and the effects of secondary trauma. Make self-care a part of your onboarding process and new teacher induction. Start the process by developing a consciousness surrounding secondary trauma, and an awareness of the importance of self-care in the lives of your new employees. Even in the interview process, have some discussion of prospective employees' views on taking care of themselves, stress, and emotional management. By doing this, you demonstrate that you value self-care and supporting your employees.

Use the first staff meeting of the new school year to focus on self-care and talk about the effects of secondary trauma and resources for working through the trauma. Send all staff weekly videos or other web links that feature wellness and self-care activities. Maybe some of your staff members can create short videos, too, sharing specific activities or approaches that help them to deal with the stress and trauma they have experienced in the classroom.

Your action plan for responding to identified needs at your school should also incorporate ongoing supports that are always in place to meet the personal and professional needs of your staff members.

Employee Assistance Programs (EAPs)

EAPs are a great resource for helping staff work through the problems that life brings, offering "free and confidential assessments, short-term counseling, referrals, and follow-up services to employees who have personal and/or work-related problems" (U.S. Office of Personnel Management, n.d.). Many people think of EAPs as being related to tragic problems or crises, but many offer counseling as part of their services. Invite your EAP provider to a staff meeting to talk about tools and resources that can help when going through tough or stressful times.

EAPs also allow staff members to seek help completely. Many of these programs have phone, telemedicine, or in-person counseling services to support the needs of educators.

Routine Wellness Assessments

Many school leaders have systems that allow them to check in on the social and emotional needs of their students (see Chapter 5), but how many do this with their educators? Consider establishing a system for conducting monthly wellness assessments. You might make it a "wellness thermometer" that you distribute at an all-staff meeting and ask attendees to use for reflection (see Figure 7.1). This confidential document will only be viewed by the principal or leadership team for the sole purpose of offering staff support. In addition, we suggest leading a discussion on the importance of self-care and

7.1 Staff Wellness Thermometer

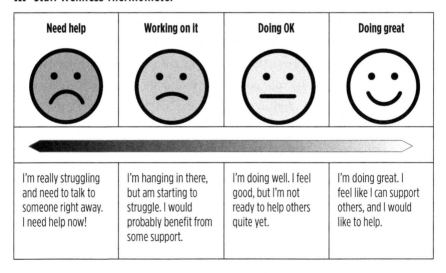

Need help	Working on it	Doing OK	Doing great
I'm really struggling and need to talk to someone right away. I need help now!	I'm hanging in there, but am starting to struggle. I would probably benefit from some support.	I'm doing well. I feel good, but I'm not ready to help others quite yet.	I'm doing great. I feel like I can support others, and I would like to help.

encouraging staff to come to the administration privately for support and help. Remind staff that these conversations will be completely confidential. Be sure to regularly share information on services available in the school and district to help staff deal with the stresses of the job, and other opportunities for counseling and support.

▶ Make It OK to Not Be OK

In earlier chapters, we addressed the fear and apprehension that create a huge hurdle for students when asking for help. It is still taboo in many respects for adults to admit that they need help or that they are struggling. There is still stigma surrounding mental and emotional health. This has improved somewhat over the years but, overall, society views mental health and physical health quite differently. We have all known people who have been injured on the job, including educators. No one blinks an eye about filling out the paperwork and getting medical treatment. On the other hand, following an emotional injury, the tendency is to soldier on and suffer in silence. This is a barrier that must be addressed—and the first thing you can do is to ensure that there is a climate of trust within your school, for both students and staff. Sharing feelings and emotions at times is a very private thing; it can be risky to open up. Nobody likes to be vulnerable. Your goal is for your staff members to understand that you are attempting to help them. That's it, no ulterior motive.

Educators need to understand that it's OK to *not* be OK. They don't need to always have the answers, be the strong ones, or just push through. Sometimes, the best thing teachers can do is to admit that they are struggling. Healing can begin only when they have the bravery to admit that they are not OK and ask for help. Let the understanding that "it's OK to not be OK" be part of your daily greeting of staff members (see Chapter 6).

Teachers generally are, by nature, fixers and doers, eager to support others. They tend not to think twice about helping someone work through a problem or complex issue or resolve a conflict. So why should they face the Goliath of secondary trauma alone? The fact is, battling secondary trauma can quickly defeat even the strongest person unless they have support and help from others. Being able to seek help strengthens the ability to work through secondary trauma and other challenges in the future and models a healthy example for others. Be sure that your teachers know how to access supports at home, in school, and in the community.

Trusted and Caring Supports

Trusted and caring supports are people who know you, care about you, and want the best for you: friends, family members, clergy. These individuals can provide a listening ear, a word of encouragement, or a tool for recovery. They are also somewhat distant from the situation and can offer a fresh perspective on the situation that you are facing.

It's also important that your teachers have trusted and caring supports at school—colleagues they can connect with to share their struggles with secondary trauma. They need to be able to turn to others and ask for help. Sometimes it can be helpful to talk to a fellow teacher in another school or district, or seek out teacher-led support groups. Andrea worked in a school where some teachers held a biweekly informal session where they sat around and just talked. This was a great time to support each other by commiserating (not complaining!) about issues in their building, what they were feeling, and brainstorming ideas to help one another cope.

Counseling

School counselors support students—but they are also wonderful at working with school employees (and they do it so much more than you think). They also are a great source for resources in the community. Outside counselors—particularly those who specialize in secondary trauma—can provide your teachers with a fresh perspective, new strategies, and links to support groups. An outside counselor also provides a level of confidentiality that often allows a teacher to speak more freely.

▶ Share Stories of the Journey

When a student at Bill's school died unexpectedly during the school year, shock and grief descended on both students and staff. During an all-staff meeting, Bill talked about losing his sister years before due to breast cancer, and how the grief overwhelmed him to the point that it was difficult for him to function, in both work and his personal life. For days, and even weeks, he remembered, he would cry on the drive to and from school. Bill acknowledged that he should have reached out for help, sought counseling, and that he would have benefited from joining a grief support group. Today, he knows, this type of grief is not something you overcome; you just learn to live through it. After the meeting, many of the staff members thanked Bill for sharing, for the transparency, and for the heartfelt focus on supporting them. When leaders share stories of their own struggles, modeling honesty and transparency, it makes it much easier for others to ask for support, help, or guidance.

You can learn so much from someone's personal growth story. Include time in faculty meetings for sharing stories from the week, about an issue they are dealing with, or how they overcame something in their lives. Focusing on the power of a story allows your staff to see that others are struggling, others are triumphing, and others are resilient just like them. "Stories emotionalize information. They give color and depth to otherwise bland material and they allow people to connect with the message in a deeper, more meaningful way" (TonyRobbins.com, 2017, para. 5).

Julie, a special education teacher, works with students who experience trauma every day. Kids in her class have experienced loss, abuse, violence, poverty, and neglect. Yet, she always comes to school with a tireless commitment to inspire her students and motivates everyone around her, staff included. Her infectious, upbeat, and positive nature brightens every room she enters and brightens the hallways of Bill's school. Julie values helping others, finds solace in spending time with her family and friends, and has a deep commitment to her faith. She's an excellent example of working through secondary trauma by accessing support and resources, and she flourishes in her work as a teacher. Bill has marveled at her ability to deal with secondary trauma and to teach with such passion and love for her students.

▶ Provide Professional Learning on Secondary Trauma

Bill's wife is a nurse; recently, she was working with COVID-19 patients at a long-term care facility. Her employer recognized the need to support the medical staff through the immense compassion fatigue and secondary trauma many were experiencing during the pandemic. The professional learning session offered gave personnel an opportunity to learn how to deal with grief, to talk about their own grief, and to hear the stories of other nurses and how they were working through their grief. There was a chaplain with whom they could talk, who encouraged them and helped them through their daily, courageous work.

Could your staff benefit from a shift away from the usual stand-and-deliver professional learning to a small-group time of sharing, reflection, and learning? Often, smaller groups are more authentic and produce much richer and deeper conversations that bring about real healing. Vary the types of professional learning you offer to support the varying needs of your staff. In Bill's school district, teachers often focus on self-care during professional learning time. Schools offer yoga classes, exercise classes, golfing, and other activities that allow staff members to refresh, recharge, and reenergize for the work ahead.

Partnerships outside your school and district can complement your program. In addition to outside counselors, representatives from local hospitals, county offices, and mental health agencies are great resources to provide professional learning and growth opportunities. Many of these professionals will do it at no or low cost. Many health professionals also offer support via telemedicine. Schools in Bill and Dave's district have had presentations and support from a variety of local professionals, including chiropractors (sending a massage therapist to provide chair massages), doctors (presentations on childhood trauma and secondary trauma), outside counselors (training, support, and counseling), and nutritionists (presentations on healthy eating).

You might also consider adding complementary activities that demonstrate awareness of the effects of secondary trauma and encourage staff to access strategies to manage it.

Monthly Mindfulness Activities

In Chapter 6, we shared some mindfulness activities that teachers could do with students. You can also design fun, upbeat, and engaging mindfulness activities and challenge staff to participate in them.

Social-emotional learning (SEL) Bingo. At Andrea's elementary school, the library media center chooses different themes each month and includes fun activities in which kids and staff can participate. For SEL Bingo, players choose different things to do to take care of their personal wellness. When they get a "bingo" from doing these activities, they turn in their sheet and receive a cute gift.

Scavenger hunts. Who doesn't like a good scavenger hunt, especially when the winning prize is really awesome? Design a scavenger hunt that requires staff to work through mindfulness activities or stations throughout the school: taking a walk around the school, listening to their favorite music, taking time to meditate, doing breathing exercises, working out in the school fitness center, or writing about their thoughts and reflections. Apps such as Goose Chase can enhance the scavenger hunt experience, allowing participants to share photos and artifacts of their hunt, and providing a leader board and point count for different experiences. You know how you really get participation? Provide the winning staff member with a vacation day or self-care day and cover their classes for the day.

Learning Alone—and Together

Many schools and districts have book clubs where faculty, staff, and students read the same book. What about starting a book club at your school, or sharing a collection of readings on this topic? Staff members can read these materials or watch videos on their own time. You might even develop digital badges for completing different stages, which both motivates participation and gives you a way to track learning. Each summer, Justin's school book club takes turns picking books to read and meets each week for discussion and breakfast at a local café. It builds community within the staff and keeps them connected when they typically wouldn't get to see each other. This year, their book club continued through the school year and meets on Friday afternoons after school.

A weekly Padlet or activity where staff can highlight some self-care idea, activities, and strategies and share them with one another fosters a community of togetherness, support, and help.

▶ Keep Building Your Community

Andrea's school uses the Leader in Me framework (https://www .leaderinme.org), which incorporates social-emotional learning, college and career readiness, and leadership training. A few times each year, her school has a "sharpen the saw" event for staff—movie nights, meals at restaurants, painting parties. Whenever staff can laugh together, they build memories and support networks that help them during the dark times of teaching.

The power of giving back can often provide some healing for those experiencing secondary trauma. Join together to help your local community. Many of Andrea's school staff members volunteer in the summer with a local nonprofit organization that works in teams to help families in need with home projects. By giving back, you get back: feelings of accomplishment, self-worth, and value. This type of self-care can be powerful, especially when a staff works together toward a common goal or project to help their community.

👥 Reflecting on Secondary Trauma

Educators have such an empathetic and compassionate nature—this is what makes them so amazing. You must protect this and be creative in connecting with, supporting, and empowering them to give their best every day.

- How will you use staff check-ins to help adults in your building self-assess their social-emotional well-being?
- What challenged your thinking? Why?
- What are your school's greatest needs regarding supporting faculty and staff through secondary trauma?
- What do you do well in supporting faculty and staff through secondary trauma? What are you most proud of?
- Who is your school's "Julie"? What can they teach you about helping staff to manage this stress successfully?

Gather your grade-level partners, school leadership team, cabinet, or any other collaborative group and discuss your reflections on the content of this chapter.

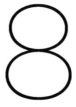

A Call to Action

Turning Trauma into Triumph

You may not always have a comfortable life and you will not always be able to solve all of the world's problems at once. But don't ever underestimate the impact you can have, because history has shown us that courage can be contagious, and hope can take on a life of its own.

———————————————

—Michelle Obama—
Remarks by the First Lady During Keynote Address at Young African Women Leaders Forum

Have faith in the fact that lives can change. Even though the darkness of trauma can have lasting effects and may appear to be overwhelming, it doesn't need to be a life sentence. In this chapter, we will share real-life stories from staff and students who have overcome their traumatic experiences to thrive in life and add a few more recommendations to this book's collection of trauma-sensitive leadership principles.

Perhaps one of the greatest missing pieces in the culture of many schools is hope. It is important to let kids know that their future is not dependent on the trauma they have faced, the obstacles before them, or the failures of their past. Just the opposite: their future is based on their hard work, dedication, and resilience. In Chapter 1, we encouraged you to accept students where they are, with their failures and insecurities, and for who they are—rather than what you think they should be. This type of unconditional love builds positive relationships with students, supporting their learning and providing benefits that go beyond learning.

Greg's Story: From Pain to Purpose

When Bill was an assistant principal, he knew a student named Greg who was struggling to gain traction and capitalize on his great potential. Greg's ongoing discipline problem made him a regular in Bill's office.

Greg came from a caring, loving, and wonderful family, led by a mom who was raising four kids in Section 8 housing with the help of her own mother and other friends and relatives. Greg's mom put a lot of value on education and was committed to seeing that her kids received a great education so they could break the chain of poverty and pursue their dreams.

As a child, Greg was close to his sister. She had cerebral palsy and faced numerous health challenges, but her spirit and smile could light up any room; they were inseparable. One Christmas morning, Greg woke up to find that his sister had died in the bed next to him. This tragedy and grief overwhelmed the family and pushed Greg into a tailspin. In middle school, Greg struggled to stay focused, get good grades, and stay out of trouble. In high school, however, he made a total transformation, vowing to turn his life around to honor his sister and to fulfill his mom's dreams.

Later in high school, Greg's grades soared as he took more rigorous courses and took on leadership roles in the school. He got involved in student government and was elected president of the student body. Greg earned a full scholarship to Syracuse University; at first, he wasn't sure if he could accept the scholarship because he didn't have transportation to and from school. Bill encouraged him to accept and pledged his support to resolve the transportation issue.

For the next four years, Bill drove Greg to and from Syracuse, a four-hour trip each way. These long drives provided an opportunity for highly engaging conversations about the future ahead. Greg graduated from Syracuse with honors, the first member of his family to graduate from college. Commencement was a special day, seeing Greg hug his mom and brothers, wearing his cap and gown. Greg's younger brother followed in his footsteps and also received the same scholarship—and Bill helped to drive him back and forth as well.

Today, Greg is a successful businessman who is giving back to his community. His story is an example of breaking the grip of trauma and turning pain into purpose, trauma into triumph. His transformation, however, was the result of many people coming together to support his growth and success. His family, friends, and educators influenced his life in a way that inspired him to face the challenges of life. Greg benefited from educators who applied the principles in this book:

- They looked behind his discipline issues and saw him—and his potential.
- They empowered him to develop his leadership skills.
- They built caring, nurturing, and positive relationships with him.
- They invested in his life beyond academics.
- They nurtured positive and caring relationships with his family.
- They were authentic, genuine, and sincere in their interactions with him and his family.
- They teamed up to support Greg and his transformation.
- They made sure that Greg was connected to at least one caring adult in the school.
- They focused on Greg's successes.

Years later, it was inspiring to witness Greg come back and talk to the student body about his experience growing up, how he was resilient, and how he overcame life's challenges to find success and flourish in life. To support students like Greg, educators can share stories of hope and inspiration, demonstrate kindness and understanding, and acknowledge these students' resilience.

▶ Help Students See Their Potential for Success

Some very successful, well-known individuals have spoken out about traumatic experiences in their lives or their own or a family member's mental health challenges. Such stories are a reminder that trauma, and its effects, can appear in the lives of all kinds of people—and that it can be overcome. Many of your students and your staff have been affected by traumatic events as children or as adults.

Inspiration from Famous Faces

In 2017, a terrorist detonated a bomb at an arena in Manchester, England, during a concert by the pop star Ariana Grande. That blast killed 22 people and injured more than 800 others. That event caused Taylor Swift to consider extra precautions for her own concert tour two years later. An article in *The Telegraph* recounted how Grande continues to face, and overcome, this tragedy: "It's hard to talk about because so many people have suffered such severe, tremendous loss. But, yeah, [PTSD] is a real thing. I don't think I'll ever know how to talk about it and not cry" (Horton, 2019).

At 13 years old, Monica Seles became the youngest professional tennis player to achieve a #1 world ranking. In 1993, she was attacked on the court, during a changeover in a match. Seles took a two-year break while receiving treatment for PTSD. She successfully returned to the professional tennis circuit for the 1995 season. Since retiring in 2008, Seles has written and spoken about PTSD and its treatment.

Charlize Theron is easily one of the most recognized and successful people in show business. When she was 15, her alcoholic father shot through the door of the room where she and her mother were hiding. Theron recalled that "none of those bullets ever hit us, which is just a miracle. But in self-defense, she ended the threat. [Theron's mother shot her father.] The more we talk about these things, the more we realize we are not alone in any of it" (BBC News, 2019). Theron has stressed that support from her mom as a key aspect that allowed her to be resilient and achieve success.

Musicians, athletes, actors, and producers—in all walks of life there are individuals with traumatic events in their past. You will certainly find people who need encouragement and care in your school. There is one thing that spans across all areas of success in curriculum, instruction, learning, assessment, discipline, and communication: relationships. Strong relationships foster and nurture the building of faith and hope. When you create these kinds of caring spaces for students in your school, the difference can last a lifetime (Jones et al., 2015).

Inspiration from Familiar Faces

Hope is not reserved for the rich and famous. Which students in your school could most use some hope and love because of their current situations? Encourage your teachers to be intentional in speaking life into these students every single day. Educators have the ability to have a lasting influence on the lives of kids.

When Andrea thinks about hope, she remembers a particular person who had very little hope as a child—a family friend, Clark. He grew up in the projects. His family had little money and there were times they had absolutely nothing to eat. When teachers talked about Clark, they probably complained about his absences and the lack of parental support. He wasn't the model student who did his homework every night. His family was very dysfunctional. There were several children, a mom who did the very best she knew how, and a dad who was an alcoholic and drug user. His interactions with his children were rarely positive, if at all. The last memory Clark had of his dad, when he was still a young boy, involved a weapon. After that traumatic experience, there were many people who rallied around Clark: teachers, community members, and church leaders. They gave him hope and encouragement.

Clark married and had children and grandchildren. He went on to serve others around the world in impoverished areas, sharing love and giving hope. He volunteered helping at-risk teenagers. He served in community outreach groups, providing food, clothing, and support to families in need. He believed in hard work: you gave nothing but your best at everything you set out to do, whether you were cleaning toilets or working beside the CEO.

There were many people along the way who had faith in Clark, showing him love and speaking hope and life into him. He broke the cycle of poverty in his family, which would not have been possible without someone breathing these positive attributes into his life. Clark passed away a few years ago, but the legacy he left made a lasting impact on Andrea's life. Because someone believed in him, he taught Andrea also how to love, lead, and serve.

▶ Have Faith in Students . . . and Share It

What might grow, years from now, because of the seeds of hope and love planted in students? Students need adults like Clark to model faith, hope, and love. They need caring adults telling them who they are and who they can be. They will live up to the expectations teachers have for them when they sense this faith and trust.

Are the students in your school reminded daily of what they can accomplish? Do they hear this faith in them, and do they see it? Many students will never hear it or see it outside the school walls.

You and your teachers need to demonstrate faith in students: faith that they will make good decisions and do the right things. Kids who have been affected by adverse childhood experiences hunger for an adult to believe and have faith in them. Nurturing a culture of trust in the classroom creates a learning environment where students thrive and flourish.

Respect and trust are foundational for learning. This is nothing new—we know it to be true. We also know that building trust is not a "one and done" kind of thing to be checked off at the beginning of the year. We need to work at it every day and maintain what we do gain. (Johnson, 2018, para. 2)

Have faith in kids, believe in them, and trust them to live out what they are taught. This isn't blind faith believing they will never make a mistake or have a mishap. Just the opposite: it's faith that knows kids are going to make mistakes. But it's also a faith that believes kids—all kids—are intrinsically good people. When you demonstrate this type of faith in kids, especially those affected by trauma, it builds independence, confidence, and a maturity to take on life's challenges.

▶ Establish Expectations

It is difficult for kids to act appropriately when they don't know what the expectations are. Work with students to build a community of set expectations for all students, and trust them to abide by these expectations. Model the behaviors you want to see, ask them to role-play with their peers, and expect them to live out these behaviors in the classroom.

> Students do not learn what's announced; they learn what they are taught. It makes no more sense to announce rules regarding acceptable student behaviors than it does to announce—rather than teach—math facts. It is critical that you formally teach and enforce both a discipline plan and rules of conduct from the very first day of school. (Boynton & Boynton, 2005, p. 23)

Nothing demonstrates faith in kids like having high expectations for them and supporting them to meet those expectations. Far too often, teachers lower their expectations, thinking that students are not capable of meeting the rigor of learning. The truth is that kids have a keen ability to meet and exceed expectations. Set high goals, and provide the resources and support to help students attain them. As Johnson (2014) points out, "We earn our students' trust by showing them respect in the form of meaningful, challenging, and rewarding learning activities that are worthy of their time and best efforts" (para. 6).

▶ Demonstrate Kindness

When Andrea was a classroom teacher, she wanted her students to value helping others without expecting anything in return and to show love to strangers. She decided to have a class giving project, which she called the "10 Days of Giving." Each day, students brought in something different to give away. They brought in socks and hats for the homeless, and lotions for residents at the local nursing home. They collected canned goods to donate to the local food pantry. At the end of the project, the class had a special breakfast together on the last day of school before the winter break. It was a great way to reflect and make a special memory together. Of course, it's important to consider that some of your students may not have anything "extra" at home to bring in and give away. An idea to support these students is for the teacher to bring in additional items that they can give to these students to help them feel like they are part of the activity.

Another way students at Andrea's school display love and kindness is to write "Nice Notes" and place them in a mailbox in the school library. Kids write these notes to other students or to staff in the building, and they are delivered once a week. Everyone looks forward to receiving one from time to time.

In Chapter 5, we described Andrea's school's "house" framework and how this has been used to improve relationships and build a positive school culture. At least one time throughout the school year, there is a house competition where kids bring in items to help a charity. Students have donated items to the local Ronald McDonald House and collected nonperishable items to add to "The Little Red House" located outside the elementary school. This is an anonymous food pantry installed by a church, where anyone can come get food for their family (as students in the school have). Teams of people from the community make sure it is restocked every day with things that kids can prepare for themselves and their siblings.

▶ Instill Hope

Perhaps one of your greatest responsibilities is to breathe hope into your students, especially those impacted by trauma. Adverse childhood experiences can negatively influence a student's trajectory and even cause biological and health issues that carry into adulthood. We have seen for ourselves just how much of a positive difference one caring and supportive adult can make in the life of children who are living with the effects of trauma. Now think about what an entire staff of such adults, dedicated to underscoring the inherent value and vast potential of these students, might achieve together.

Speaking Life into Others

"Speaking life into" someone means being encouraging, uplifting, and inspiring—not in a toxic-positive way that ignores trauma but in a way that encourages a student and speaks words of hope and inspiration. *Toxic positivity* "refers to the concept that keeping positive, and keeping positive only, is the right way to live your life. It means only focusing on positive things and rejecting anything that may trigger negative emotions" (Lukin, 2019, para. 2).

Speaking life into someone recognizes the challenges they are facing or have faced and the obstacles that they need to overcome. It means speaking words of hope into their lives, words that are backed up and supported by a genuine focus on caring for the individual. Kids affected by trauma already have heard what they are doing wrong—tell them what they are doing well.

Valuing Students as Whole People

Educators can fall into the trap of valuing kids for what they do rather than for who they are. The teacher's pet, the coach's best player, the director's state-qualifying musician, the high achiever—all these distinctions are based on actions. Focus on kids for who they are, not for what they can do. Only valuing kids for what they do alienates those who are struggling, failing, misbehaving, or withdrawn. Many of these kids have experienced trauma.

Valuing students for who they are also demonstrates unconditional love, communicating that you will care for them, support them, and love them regardless of what they do. Your love for them is not conditional on their *actions* but on who they are as a person. Madeline Will's (2020) article in *EdWeek* shares how educators can work to value each student and to love the unlovable. She recommends not taking things personally and finding something to like in each student, to open up with students to build connection, build a positive classroom culture, and nurture a positive relationship with parents. She also reminds us to not expect instant results as working with students can take more time than we would like.

Just Being There

To instill hope, you must commit to being there for kids. When they make mistakes, do something stupid, or fail miserably, you are still there to support and accompany them. Don't blow up, give them the silent treatment, withdraw, blame them, or get accusatory. Just the opposite: embrace them, draw close, and guide them through getting back on the right track.

When Bill was in college, he accidentally drove the family car through the garage doors. It ripped the garage door off the hinges and caused a lot of damage to the frame. Panicking, Bill called a friend who was a contractor to see if it could be fixed before his dad got home. (It couldn't.) But to Bill's surprise, his dad wasn't angry at all. He was more worried about Bill than he was about the garage doors: "Son, I can replace garage doors; I can't replace you. I'm just glad you are all right."

This is the attitude that kids who are affected by trauma need demonstrated: someone is here for you, regardless of what you do. It's reassurance, and it's hope. It helps them understand that mistakes can be overcome, and errors can be forgiven and forgotten.

👥 Reflecting on Overcoming Trauma

A student who has an educator in their life who demonstrates faith, hope, and love for them can help them overcome the challenges trauma brings. Much like Greg, Clark, Monica, Charlize, and many others, your students can turn their trauma into triumph and pain into purpose with the support of loving and supportive caring adults. Are you doing everything you can to help your students overcome trauma?

- Have you shared stories of turning pain into purpose or trauma into triumph with your team members?
- Are you sharing stories of overcoming with students?
- Do students have examples of people overcoming obstacles, in your school?

- Do your teachers and other staff members demonstrate their faith in kids to do the right thing?
- How are you modeling love for kids?
- How are you instilling hope into the lives of kids?

Gather your grade-level partners, school leadership team, cabinet, or any other collaborative group and discuss your reflections on the content of this chapter.

Acknowledgments

We want to acknowledge all the students, teachers, and families we have been honored to serve as educational leaders. When life knocked you down, you had the courage and tenacity to stand back up. When you were blessed, you shared your abundance with others. The stories of your lives have made us better educators, leaders, and human beings. We are inspired to continue the work so every student and adult in our care can learn and thrive—now and throughout their lives.

We also want to express our deepest gratitude to Susan Hills and the entire editorial team at ASCD for empowering us to inspire educational leaders to build resilient and trauma-informed schools throughout the world.

Bill Ziegler

My family inspires me every day to be resilient, dream big, and love others. Thanks to my parents and sister for believing in me when I didn't believe in myself. You modeled resilience, taught me kindness, and demonstrated unconditional love. Dave and Hannah, you make my heart smile every day, and I will always love you. Kim, I'm blessed beyond measure to be married to you. I so appreciate your unwavering support, encouragement, and love.

Dave Ramage

Thanks to my parents, wise mentors, my amazing wife, Diane, and my children, I have the support and encouragement to lead adults and children who did not escape trauma in their formative years. I especially want to thank the students who are vulnerable enough to share their invisible stories. You help me see. I am humbled and honored to answer the call and continue caring for students and adults in the leadership spaces I tend.

Andrea Parson

I am blessed with so many wonderful family members and friends who cheer me on! To my husband: You have always inspired me to reach higher, dream big dreams, laugh more, and serve more. I love you with all that I am. To our son, Ryan: You have such a courageous spirit. May you always know and believe that you can do anything. To my late dad, Jed; my mom, Joyce; my sister, Laura; and my wonderful in-laws, Billy and Patsy: Thank you for modeling true kindness, service, and love for others. Love is the difference.

Justin Foster

I would like to acknowledge my daughters, Symone and Averie Foster, for inspiring me to always look up when things are tough and to keep working hard.

I would also like to thank my parents. My father, the late James Foster Jr., and my mother, Jamelle, instilled in me the importance of treating everyone, no matter who they are, with kindness, respect, and dignity. Thank you for always being there when I needed you and for giving me the best upbringing anyone could ask for.

References

Ablon, J. S. (2020, January 9). School discipline is trauma-insensitive and trauma-uninformed: Why change is needed to meet the needs of students exposed to trauma. *Psychology Today*. https://www.psychologytoday.com/us/blog/changeable/202001/school-discipline-is-trauma-insensitive-and-trauma-uninformed

Ablon, J. S., & Pollastri, A. R. (2018). *The school discipline fix*. Norton.

Alber, R. (2018, April 18). *When teachers experience empathetic distress*. Edutopia. https://www.edutopia.org/article/when-teachers-experience-empathic-distress

American Society for the Positive Care of Children. (2021). *Child maltreatment statistics*. https://americanspcc.org/child-abuse-statistics/

Anderson, M. (2016). *Learning to choose, choosing to learn: The key to student motivation and achievement*. ASCD.

Baicker, K. (2020, March 15). The impact of secondary trauma on educators. *ASCD Express, 15*(13).

BBC News. (2019, December 17). Charlize Theron "not ashamed" to talk about her mum killing her dad. BBC Newsbeat. http://www.bbc.com/news/newsbeat-50821672.

Boynton, M., & Boynton, C. (2005). *The educator's guide to preventing and solving discipline problems*. ASCD.

Brown, P., Roedinger, H., & McDaniel, M. (2014). *Make it stick: The science of successful learning*. Belknap Press. https://doi.org/10.4159/9780674419377

California School Boards Association. (2013, Summer). A conversation with Nadine Burke-Harris M.D. *California Schools*. https://www.csba.org/Newsroom/CASchoolsMagazine/2013/Summer/InThisIssue/2013_SummerCSM_Convo.aspx

Carter, R. T. (2007). Racism and psychological and emotional injury: Recognizing and assessing race-based traumatic stress. *The Counseling Psychologist, 35*(1), 13–105. https://doi.org/10.1177/0011000006292033

CAST. (2018). *Universal design for learning guidelines version 2.2.* http://udlguidelines.cast.org

Collaborative for Academic, Social, and Emotional Learning. (2021). *SEL: What are the core competence areas and where are they promoted?* https://casel.org/sel-framework/

Cox, J. (2021). *How to build trust with students.* Western Governors University. https://www.wgu.edu/heyteach/article/how-build-trust-students1808.html

Dhaliwal, T., (2020). *Educator bias is associated with racial disparities in student achievement and discipline.* https://www.brookings.edu/blog/brown-center-chalkboard/2020/07/20/educator-bias-is-associated-with-racial-disparities-in-student-achievement-and-discipline/

Diehm, R., & Roland, D. (2015). The impact of secondary exposure to trauma on mental health professionals. *InPsych, 37*(1).

Edwards, C. (2020). Racial truth & reconciliation: Resources & definitions. *Voices for Virginia's Children.* https://vakids.org/our-news/blog/racial-truth-reconciliation-resources-definitions

Felitti, V., Anda, R., Nordenberg, D., Williamson, D., Spitz, A., Edwards, V., Koss, M., & Marks, J. (1999). Relationship of childhood abuse and household dysfunction to many of the leading causes of death in adults: The adverse childhood experiences (ACE) study. *American Journal of Preventive Medicine, 14*(4), 245–258. https://doi.org/10.1016/S0749-3797(98)00017-8

Ferlazzo, L. (2019, September 18). I don't see color in education means I don't see you unless you act like me. *Education Week.* https://www.edweek.org/teaching-learning/opinion-i-dont-see-color-in-education-means-i-dont-see-you-unless-you-act-like-me/2019/09

Fritzgerald, A. (2020). *Antiracism and universal design for learning: Building expressways to success.* CAST.

Gaffney, C. (2019, Summer). When schools cause trauma. *Teaching Tolerance, 62.* https://www.learningforjustice.org/magazine/summer-2019/when-schools-cause-trauma

Gawlinski, A., & Steers, N. (2005). *Dogs ease anxiety, improve health status of hospitalized heart failure patients.* American Heart Association Abstract 2513. https://www.uclahealth.org/pac/Workfiles/volunteering/PACArticle.pdf

Gershenson, S., & Papageorge, N. (2021). The power of teacher expectations. *Education Next, 21*(4). https://www.educationnext.org/power-of-teacher-expectations-racial-bias-hinders-student-attainment/

Getz, L. (2011). The power of play therapy. *Social Work Today, 11*(3), 20.

Gil, E. (2010). *Working with children to heal interpersonal trauma: The power of play.* Guilford.

Ginsburg, K. (2015). *Building resilience in children and teens: Giving kids roots and wings* (3rd ed.). American Academy of Pediatrics.

Gladwell, M. (2007). *Blink: The power of thinking without thinking.* Back Bay Books.

Gorski, P. (2020, October). How trauma-informed are we, really? *Educational Leadership, 78*(2), 14–19.

Harvard Graduate School of Education. (2021). *Relationship mapping strategy.* https://mcc.gse.harvard.edu/resources-for-educators/relationship-mapping-strategy

Hattie, J., & Yates, G. (2014). *Visible learning and the science of how we learn.* Routledge.

Hess, A. J. (2019, August 9). *50% of teachers surveyed say they've considered quitting, blaming pay, stress and lack of respect.* CNBC. https://www.cnbc.com/2019/08/09/50percent-of-teachers-surveyed-say-theyve-considered-quitting-teaching.html

Horton, H. (2019, March 6). Taylor Swift reveals that she carries army grade wound dressings following Manchester Arena bombing. *The Telegraph.* https://www.telegraph.co.uk/news/2019/03/06/taylor-swift-reveals-carries-army-grade-wound-dressings-following/

Ingersoll, R. M., Merrill, E., Stuckey, D., & Collins, G. (2018). Seven trends: The transformation of the teaching force—updated October 2018. *CPRE Research Reports.* https://repository.upenn.edu/cpre_researchreports/108

Jensen, E. (2009). *Teaching with poverty in mind: What being poor does to kids' brains and what schools can do about it.* ASCD.

Jensen, E. (2016). *Poor students, rich teaching: Mindsets for change.* Solution Tree.

Johnson, B. (2014, August 7). *Developing students' trust: The key to a learning partnership.* Edutopia. https://www.edutopia.org/blog/student-trust-ben-johnson

Jones, D., Greenberg, M., & Crowley, M. (2015). Social-emotional functioning and public health: The relationship between kindergarten competence and future wellness. *American Journal of Public Health, 105*(11), 2283–2290. https://doi.org/10.2105/AJPH.2015.302630

Knost, L. R. (2013). *Whispers through time: Communication through the ages and stages of childhood.* Little Hearts Books.

Lave, J., & Wenger, E. (1991). *Situated learning: Legitimate peripheral participation.* Cambridge University Press.

Leeb, R. T., Bitsko, R. H., Radhakrishnan, L., Martinez, P., Njai, R., Holland, K. M. (2020, November 13). Mental health–related emergency department visits among children aged <18 years during the COVID-19 pandemic—United States, January 1–October 17, 2020. *MMWR, 69,* 1675–1680. http://dx.doi.org/10.15585/mmwr.mm6945a3

Ludy-Dobson, C., & Perry, B. D. (2010). The role of healthy relational interactions in buffering the impact of childhood trauma. In E. Gil (Ed.). *Working with children to heal interpersonal trauma* (pp. 26–44). Guilford.

Lukin, K. (2019, August 1). Toxic positivity: Don't always look on the bright side. *Psychology Today.* https://www.psychologytoday.com/us/blog/the-man-cave/201908/toxic-positivity-dont-always-look-the-bright-side

Minahan, J. (2020, July 1). *Maintaining connections, reducing anxiety while school is closed* (*Educational Leadership* Special Report). https://www.ascd.org/el/articles/maintaining-connections-reducing-anxiety-while-school-is-closed

Morrison, N. (2019, June 27). Number of teachers quitting the classroom after just one year hits all-time high. *Forbes.* https://www.forbes.com/sites/nickmorrison/2019/06/27/number-of-teachers-quitting-the-classroom-after-just-one-year-hits-all-time-high/?sh=71f84d2760e5

Murray, T. C. (2019). *Personal & authentic: Designing learning experiences that impact a lifetime.* Impress.

National Alliance on Mental Illness. (2022). *Mental health screening.* https://www.nami.org/Advocacy/Policy-Priorities/Improving-Health/Mental-Health-Screening

National Child Traumatic Stress Network. (n.d.). *Complex trauma.* https://www
.nctsn.org/what-is-child-trauma/trauma-types/complex-trauma

National Child Traumatic Stress Network. (2018). *Creating school active shooter/
intruder drills.* https://www.nctsn.org/sites/default/files/resources/fact-sheet
/creating_school_active_shooter_intruder_drills.pdf

Obama, M. (2011, June 22). *Remarks by the first lady during keynote address at Young
African Women Leaders Forum.* https://obamawhitehouse.archives.gov
/the-press-office/2011/06/22/remarks-first-lady-during-keynote-address
-young-african-women-leaders-fo

Partnership for 21st Century Skills. (2002). *Learning for the 21st century: A report
and MILE guide for 21st century skills.* https://eric.ed.gov/?id=ED480035

Ruland, S. (2019, June 19). How a bald pageant contestant tackled her depression to
compete for Miss Pennsylvania. *York Daily Record.* https://www.ydr.com
/story/news/2019/06/19/miss-pennsylvania-2019-central-pa-sarah
-pennington-mental-health-advocate-conversation/1472469001/

Sacks, V., & Murphey, D. (2018). *The prevalence of adverse childhood experiences,
nationally, by state, and by race or ethnicity.* Child Trends. Available online at:
https://www.childtrends.org/publications/prevalence-adverse-childhood
-experiences-nationally-state-race-ethnicity

Schulman, M., & Maul, A. (2019, February). *Screening for adverse childhood experiences and trauma.* https://www.chcs.org/resource/screening-for-adverse
-childhood-experiences-and-trauma/

Seeley-Brown, J., & Duguid, P. (2002). *The social life of information.* Harvard Business School.

Souers, K., & Hall, P. (2020, October). Trauma is a word—not a sentence. *Educational
Leadership, 78*(2), 34–39.

Sparks, D. (2018, September 12). Mayo Mindfulness: Practicing mindfulness exercises. *Mayo Clinic News Network.* https://newsnetwork.mayoclinic.org
/discussion/mayo-mindfulness-practicing-mindfulness-exercises/

Starck, J., Riddle, T., Sinclair, S., & Warikoo, N. (2020). Teachers are people too:
Examining the racial bias of teachers compared to other American adults.
Educational Researcher, 49(4), 273–284. https://doi.org/10.3102/0013189
X20912758

Tatum, B. (2017). *Why are all the black kids sitting together in the cafeteria?* Basic
Books.

Tatum, B. D. (n.d.). *Color blind or color conscious? How schools acknowledge racial
and ethnic identities will affect all students' educational experiences.* AASA.
https://www.aasa.org/SchoolAdministratorArticle.aspx?id=14892

Thiers, N. (2020, October). Turn and talk: Nadine Burke Harris on responding to
student trauma. *Educational Leadership, 78*(2), 12–13.

Tomlinson, C. A. (2017). *How to differentiate instruction in academically diverse classrooms* (3rd ed.). ASCD.

Tomlinson, C. A. (2020, October). Learning from kids who hurt. *Educational Leadership, 78*(2), 28–33.

TonyRobbins.com. (2017, April 4) *How to be more persuasive in business and in life,
according to a Hollywood exec who's spent 30 years making people care.* Business
Insider. https://www.businessinsider.com/tony-robbins-peter-guber-advice
-for-persuasion-2016-4

Trossman, R., Spence, S.-L., Mielke, J. G., & McAuley, T. (2021). How do adverse childhood experiences impact health? Exploring the mediation role of executive functions. *Psychological Trauma: Theory, Research, Practice, and Policy*, *13*(2), 206–213. https://doi.org/10.1037/tra0000965

UCLA School of Health. (2020). *Animal assisted therapy research*. https://www.uclahealth.org/pac/animal-assisted-therapy

University of Portsmouth. (2020, December 10). Robots could replace real therapy dogs. *International Journal of Social Robotics*. https://www.eurekalert.org/news-releases/665918

U.S. Office of Personnel Management. (n.d.). *Frequently asked questions: What is an Employee Assistance Program (EAP)?* https://www.opm.gov/faqs/QA.aspx?fid=4313c618-a96e-4c8e-b078-1f76912a10d9&pid=2c2b1e5b-6ff1-4940-b478-34039a1e1174

Usher, K. (2019, April 10). *Differentiating by offering choices*. Edutopia. https://www.edutopia.org/article/differentiating-offering-choices

van der Kolk, B. (2014). *The body keeps the score: Brain, mind, and body in the healing of trauma*. Penguin Books.

Vincenty, S. (2020, June 12). *Being "color blind" doesn't make you not racist—In fact, it can mean the opposite*. Oprah Daily. https://www.oprahdaily.com/life/relationships-love/a32824297/color-blind-myth-racism

Will, M. (2020, June 9). Teachers are as racially biased as everybody else, study shows. *EdWeek*. https://www.edweek.org/teaching-learning/teachers-are-as-racially-biased-as-everybody-else-study-shows/2020/06

Ziegler, W., & Ramage, D. (2017). *Future focused leaders: Relate, innovate and invigorate for real educational change*. Corwin. https://doi.org/10.4135/9781071801413

Ziegler, W., & Ramage, D. (2020). *You don't need superpowers to be a student's hero: Leading a hero-building school culture*. Corwin.

Index

The letter *f* following a page locator denotes a figure.

About the Authors

BILL ZIEGLER, EdD, has worked in public education for more than 27 years as a teacher, assistant
principal, and principal. He is a national speaker
and podcast host (Lead the Way EDU), and the
coauthor of *Future-Focused Leaders: Relate, Innovate, and Invigorate for Real Educational Change*
(2017) and *You Don't Need Superpowers to Be a Kid's Hero: Leading a
Hero-Building School Culture* (2020). He served as treasurer for the
National Association of Secondary School Principals (NASSP) and
as a member of the Apple Distinguished Schools Advisory Board.

Bill has been honored as the 2016 Pennsylvania Principal of
the Year and the 2015 NASSP Digital Award Winner, was selected
to serve on the United States team of school leaders to the Great
Leaders Summit in China in 2015, and helped to rewrite the NASSP
Breaking Ranks publications for school leaders. He is an Apple

Distinguished Educator and the former cohost of the #AppleEDU-LeaderChat on Twitter.

Bill earned his doctorate degree from Temple University, where he currently serves as an adjunct professor in the Masters of Education program. He and his beautiful wife, Kim, have two children.

Bill can often be found fly fishing in the streams of Pennsylvania, cheering on his favorite Philly sports teams, or playing his saxophone. He can be reached on Twitter and Instagram (@drbillziegler) or via a call or text on his cell phone at 610-312-9245.

DAVE RAMAGE, PhD, has been a public school educator for more than 30 years. He started as a middle school music teacher, later moving into an instructional coach role and working as a staff developer. Dave has also served in middle school assistant principal and principal roles, has done graduate teaching for several universities, and currently serves Pottsgrove School District as the Director of Integration for Learning and Instruction. He is excited to lead and grow a learning community that improves instruction, innovates with technology, values critical thinking, and cares for the growth of every student.

Dave was a 2005 national finalist in *Technology & Learning* magazine's Technology Leaders Award. He has presented at conferences including PETE&C, NECC, ISTE, PASCD, and the National Principals Conference, and he is the coauthor of *Future Focused Leaders* (2017) and *You Don't Need Superpowers to be a Kid's Hero* (2020). He became an Apple Distinguished Educator in 2019 and eagerly looks for ways to help school leaders use technology to enhance and expand the ways they approach learning.

Dave and his wife, Diane, have three children who currently practice their lifelong learning as professor, teacher, and grad student. Dave loves to make music—especially playing bass with his friends. When road conditions permit, you'll find him on two wheels carving up some of the great roads in the Northeast. Follow Dave on Twitter @DrDaveRamage.

 **ANDREA PARSON** is a school counselor at Cumberland County Elementary School in Burkesville, Kentucky. She has served at the elementary level since 2005 as a classroom teacher, library media specialist, and school counselor. She was a 2009 Mickelson Exxon Mobil National Educator and a Kentucky Teacher of the Year nominee in 2012 and 2013. She is a Youth Mental Health First Aid national trainer. As a regular presenter across the region, Andrea has most recently presented at the Kentucky P3 Project Conference as well as The Leader in Me Symposium. Her passion for outreach and helping children has taken her around the globe, serving all over the United States and Africa. Andrea and her husband, Tim (also a leader in education), have a son, Ryan, and a goldendoodle named Toby. Andrea has a passion for raising autism awareness in honor of their son. In her spare time, she loves to sing, travel, and check off family bucket-list items. Andrea believes in the importance of relationships, service, and the power of simple acts of kindness.

 **JUSTIN FOSTER** is an experienced school counselor who specializes in the whole child and interventions for students and teachers. Justin enjoys talking with others about ways they can connect, teach, and lead students from diverse backgrounds.

Throughout his career in education, Justin has worked in various settings from high school to his current assignment as an elementary school counselor. He also continues to work (as he has for over 20 years) as a community mental health therapist working with children and their families who have experienced trauma. Justin is passionate about the importance of taking care of one's mind, body, and spirit, and how this connection is essential for total health and fitness. Justin loves the outdoors, doing anything and everything from running and biking to horseback riding. One of Justin's favorite things to remind his students is to work hard and be kind.

Related ASCD Resources: Trauma-Informed Practice

At the time of publication, the following resources were available (ASCD stock numbers in parentheses):

Better Than Carrots or Sticks: Restorative Practices for Better Classroom Management by Dominique Smith, Douglas B. Fisher, and Nancy E. Frey (#116005)

Fostering Resilient Learners: Strategies for Creating a Trauma-Sensitive Classroom by Kristin Souers and Pete Hall (#116014)

The Formative Five: Fostering Grit, Empathy, and Other Success Skills Every Student Needs by Thomas Hoerr (#116043)

Teaching to Strengths: Supporting Students Living with Trauma, Violence, and Chronic Stress by Debbie Zacarian, Lourdes Alvarez-Ortiz, and Judie Haynes (#117035)

Relationship, Responsibility, and Regulation: Trauma-Invested Practices for Fostering Resilient Learners by Kristin Van Marter Souers and Pete Hall (#119027)

Creating a Trauma-Sensitive Classroom (QRG) by Kristin Souers and Pete Hall (#QRG118054)

Integrating SEL into Everyday Instruction (QRG) by Nancy Frey, Dominique Smith, and Douglas Fisher (#QRG119030)

All Learning Is Social and Emotional by Nancy Frey, Douglas Fisher, and Dominique Smith (#119033)

Restoring Students' Innate Power: Trauma-Responsive Strategies for Teaching Multilingual Newcomers by Louise El Yaafouri (#122004)

Taking Social-Emotional Learning Schoolwide by Thomas R. Hoerr (#120014)

Trauma-Informed Teaching and IEPs: Strategies for Building Student Resilience by Melissa Sadin (#122026)

Trauma-Invested Practices to Meet Students' Needs (QRG) by Kristin Van Marter Souers and Pete Hall (#QRG119077)

Your Students, My Students, Our Students: Rethinking Equitable and Inclusive Classrooms by Lee Ann Jung, Nancy Frey, Douglas Fisher, and Julie Kroener (# 119019)

Mindfulness in the Classroom by Thomas Hoerr (#120018)

Well-Being in Schools: Three Forces That Will Uplift Your Students in a Volatile World by Andy Hargreaves and Dennis Shirley (#122025)

For up-to-date information about ASCD resources, go to www.ascd.org. You can search the complete archives of *Educational Leadership* at www.ascd.org/el and keep up with the latest ideas, news, and solutions on the ASCD Blog at www.ascd.org/blogs.

For more information, send an email to member@ascd.org; call 1-800-933-2723 or 703-578-9600; or send a fax to 703-575-5400.

THE WHOLE CHILD

The ASCD Whole Child approach is an effort to transition from a focus on narrowly defined academic achievement to one that promotes the long-term development and success of all children. Through this approach, ASCD supports educators, families, community members, and policymakers as they move from a vision about educating the whole child to sustainable, collaborative actions.

Trauma-Sensitive School Leadership supports the **safe**, **engaged**, and **supported** tenets.

For more about the ASCD Whole Child approach, visit **www.ascd.org/wholechild.**

WHOLE CHILD
TENETS

1 HEALTHY
Each student enters school healthy and learns about and practices a healthy lifestyle.

2 SAFE
Each student learns in an environment that is physically and emotionally safe for students and adults.

3 ENGAGED
Each student is actively engaged in learning and is connected to the school and broader community.

4 SUPPORTED
Each student has access to personalized learning and is supported by qualified, caring adults.

5 CHALLENGED
Each student is challenged academically and prepared for success in college or further study and for employment and participation in a global environment.